DATE DUE

DEMCO 38-296

Land before Honour

R

Land before Honour
Palestinian Women in the
Occupied Territories

Kitty Warnock

Monthly Review Press

ition Data

HQ1728.5. Z8 W478 1990
Warnock, Kitty.   n in the occupied
Land before honour :
Palestinian women in the   N 0–85345–810–3 (pbk) : $13.00
occupied territories   Bank—Interviews.   2. Women,
                                     ews.   3. Jewish–Arab

           HQ1728.5.Z8W478   1990
           305.4′095695′3—dc20   89–13852
                                                                   CIP

Monthly Review Press
122 West 27th Street
New York, N.Y. 10001

Printed in Great Britain

10 9 8 7 6 5 4 3 2 1

Contents

Acknowledgements

My thanks first to all the women in the West Bank and Gaza Strip who offered me hospitality and devoted hours of their time to talking to me, often sharing very private and painful experiences. I was not able to quote from all of them, but every one contributed new insights into my picture of women's lives in the occupied territories. Second, to the friends without whose enthusiasm, much-needed encouragement and advice the book could not have been written – principally Daoud Abdullah, Hala Salem, and Hanan Abu Ghosh. They arranged introductions, accompanied me on my visits up and down the country, explained things I didn't understand, and acted as interpreters when necessary. Third, to friends in Britain who gave invaluable support and editorial advice at various stages: Alison Kelly, Wendy Lee, Amanda Mitchison, Helen O'Connell and Peter Syme. And lastly, to Birzeit University in the West Bank and War on Want in London, for being sympathetic employers throughout the time I was working on the book.

KITTY WARNOCK

Preface

This book grew out of the four and a half years I spent living and working in the Palestinian West Bank under Israeli occupation. The germ of the book was a simple observation: the striking contrasts between the lives of many Palestinian mothers and those of their daughters. Women with no formal education whose lives have been bounded by family, fields and flocks, have daughters studying physics in the United States or dentistry in the Soviet Union. Mothers who without protest married their cousins at the age of thirteen now find themselves sustaining their daughters through years of bitter punishment in prison for resistance against Israeli occupation. Many who were brought up to believe women should be neither seen nor heard now accept the younger generation leading national organisations and holding responsible positions in public life. Within the space of a generation, the position of women and their perceptions of themselves have been transformed. Gradual change would have occurred even in peaceful circumstances, but for Palestinians the process has been intensified and accelerated by the tragic upheavals and pressures they have experienced throughout the twentieth century.

As soon as I began to look among my friends for mother-and-daughter pairs to illustrate a short article I was thinking of writing, the project mushroomed and took on a momentum of its own. Women of all ages, I found, were in a process of examining and assessing their lives. Individually and collectively they were seeking their identities, as women and as Palestinians. As women they have experienced oppression and deprivation within their families; as Palestinians, they have experienced national disasters and the loss of their inherited world, grief, poverty, humiliation and political tyranny. Now the values on which the older generation built their lives are being called into question by social and economic changes, growing political and social awareness, and new opportunities for the young. Older women are having to seek anew the meaning and justification of their sufferings. Younger women are exploring how to take advantage of new possibilities, how to seize the initiative and create a new place for women in the future. All are eager to explain their lives, affirm their pride in their achievements, and seek support for their new demands.

As I went further, the experiences I was exploring began to appear increasingly complex. Why did a heroic political activist accept such narrow constraints on her social life? How did a poor and ill-treated peasant woman maintain such dignity and self-respect? How could one woman express in the same breath glowing nostalgia for the past and horror at its tyrannies? Or how could approval of the traditional subordination of women coexist with admiration for exceptional and heroic individuals?

For Palestinians, the intensity of many of these paradoxes can be attributed to their national history. This is what causes the combinations of acute suffering with courageous determination, of clinging attachment to the past with conscious commitment to building a future, of longing for individual fulfilment with sacrifice for the national cause. The situation of occupation and the Palestinian method of resistance, as many commentators have pointed out, invest the most private and domestic experiences with historic significance.

Palestinian women's view of themselves assumes that women's progress is so linked to the nation's progress that one cannot happen without the other. This assumption gives women a powerful sense of the significance of everything they do, and they are confident that they, and the Palestinian people as a whole, are progressing from the oppression and humiliations of the past and present to dignity and independence in the not too distant future.

Palestinians always offer hospitality to visitors, and a welcome to journalists and writers. I was privileged to have many contacts with a wide range of people all over the West Bank and Gaza Strip, through my students and their families, colleagues, neighbours, friends, and the women's committees. I had plenty of time to follow up these introductions, because Birzeit University, where I was teaching, was closed by the Israeli military authorities for months at a time every year of my stay. I was able to interview over fifty women at length, sometimes for whole days, sometimes on several separate occasions. I tried to find women who had lived in particular circumstances or had particular types of experience; but of course chance and personal inclination dictated the final selection of women I met, and though I do not think most of them were unusual, I would not claim that they are 'representative' of more than themselves.

I was engaged with the personal story, the specificity of the experience, of each woman I interviewed. Much of the individual interest and drama of individuals' lives and self-representations, with all their contradictions and accidents, has inevitably been lost in turning the interviews into a book which tries to lay out themes and issues along general lines. I hope I have not distorted, simplified and interpreted too much. I have tried to describe a starting point in time, quite arbitrarily taken as corresponding with the earliest memories of the women I met, and from there to trace economic and social changes through individual interviews. Women's resistance activity and its impact on their social status, and the organised women's movement have been treated in separate chapters.

Some readers will feel that I have devoted too little space to the subject of daily life under occupation and its particular pressure on women. Whole books could be written cataloguing the tedious litany of the Israeli authorities' behaviour towards Palestinians – brutality and racist arrogance, hypocrisy, Kafkaesque administrative traps and travesties of justice – and the humiliation, grief and anger (but hardly ever despair) that Palestinians suffer.

I was not concerned primarily with politics, and am certainly not intending to plead for the Palestinian cause: the reader will soon see that I take for granted Palestinians' right to national self-determination and to the establishment of some reasonably just way of living with Israelis. Nor was I attempting a serious study of women's role in the Palestinian national movement and resistance, though this is a subject of great interest. As it happened, during the years I was in the West Bank (1981–6) the political initiative was held by Palestinians in exile, and resistance in the occupied territories was of secondary importance. It was the period of Israel's most serious invasion of Lebanon (June 1982), the massacres of Sabra and Shatila (September 1982), the subsequent divisions and difficulties as the Palestine Liberation Organisation (PLO) struggled to re-establish some substance and leverage in international affairs after its evacuation from Beirut. The *intifada*, the uprising in which Palestinians in the occupied territories made the world listen to them and put Israel on the defensive, began two years after I left.

A Palestinian woman would have written a different book from mine, but I do not think that being a foreigner was entirely a disadvantage. My original idea, impressionistic and rather 'picturesque', was a foreigner's idea and would not perhaps have struck a Palestinian as interesting. Once I had got beyond it, the distance between me and the interviewees was probably not much more than would have been the case for a Palestinian if she was an urban bourgeois woman, or one who had been educated abroad.

At first I did wonder sometimes whether I was being treated to some sort of instinctive propaganda display put on for foreigners. I could not believe that so many women would accept the sufferings of defeat, dispersal and occupation with so much strength and pride, sustained for so many years only by their conviction of the justice of their cause. But I realised that their defiance was real: there is a communal language of images, attitudes and phrases, which supports individuals in their sufferings, turns their private grief to public strength, and is a powerful weapon of Palestinians' resistance. A Palestinian woman would have heard the same boasted readiness to suffer more, the same willingness to wait 'one hundred years or more' for justice.

I have been asked why I did not talk to Israeli women as well as Palestinians. This question comes from people who do not know the absolute separateness, physical and cultural, of the two communities. My answer is that, though there would be interesting links to be drawn between Jewish Israeli women and Palestinian women inside Israel, there would be little point in making comparisons between them and Palestinians in the occupied territories. There is very little connection between the two peoples. This has been due partly to deliberate Israeli policy, partly to fear. Official Israeli government policy has been that the occupied territories are permanently part of Israel, but this has not resulted in attempts to integrate them except as economic dependencies. If one were writing about South Africa, dramatic contrasts could illuminate the way white people live directly on the backs of black people. But Israel's exploitation of the occupied territories is much less total and less direct; for the majority on both sides there is little contact.

It would be hard to say how much the social aspirations of Palestinian women may have been influenced by Israeli women, after the familiar pattern of the conquered adopting the culture of the conquerors. Palestinians do not consciously use Israeli society as a reference and model for themselves. It is sometimes said that Palestinian men who work inside Israel are influenced by what they see of the Israeli way of life; but this influence works both ways, reinforcing attachment to Palestinian tradition as much as showing an attractive alternative. For most Palestinian women, the only Israelis they ever meet are the soldiers who come to threaten and intimidate them. Palestinian women looking for models of a progressive liberated life are more likely to look towards Jordan, Egypt and the Gulf countries, or to Eastern and Western Europe and the United States. But they do not need outside models to define their aspirations. From their own experiences they know that they want much the same things as other people do: education, work, happy marriages, freedom from social constraints, the power to contribute to their people's development and political progress, and the right to bring up their families free from fear and oppression.

Glossary of Arabic words used in the text

abu   Father.
dabke   Traditional Palestinian dance.
daya   Traditional midwife.
dinar   Jordanian currency unit, equivalent at the time of the interviews to approximately £2.00 sterling. It has continued in use in the West Bank during the occupation because it has been a much more stable currency than the Israeli shekel, and many Palestinian institutions and businesses have had their banking facilities in Amman, Jordan.

feda'i, feda'iye (f.),
feda'iin (m. pl.)   Guerrilla, freedom fighter.

hamouleh,
hamayel (pl.)   Often translated as tribe or clan, the word has no exact equivalent in English. A hamouleh is a patrilineal, patriarchal group of families claiming descent from a common ancestor, sometimes a century ago, sometimes more.

haram   Forbidden, improper (of behaviour).
'iib   Shame; something which is forbidden by religion or by custom and the honour code.
imam   Religious official, whose duties include leading prayers, preaching, and marriage ceremonies.
intifada   Uprising (literally, shaking up). The name given to the uprising in the occupied territories which began in December 1987.
jilbaab   A long, long-sleeved unbelted dress for men or women. The word is often used to refer to the

new type of overdress worn by women followers of the Islamic revival, which is made from a plain and sober-coloured fabric.

kefiyye   A checked men's headscarf. Always worn by Yaser Arafat, the *kefiyye* has become a symbol of the Palestinian nation, though it is also worn by men in some other Arab countries.

khabi   A bin which used to be built of mud and straw for storing grain indoors.

kiswe   Gifts traditionally given as part of wedding preparations by the groom to the family of the bride; often clothes or lengths of cloth.

mahr   Dower, bride-price. The gift given to the family of the bride by the family of the groom. The amount of *mahr* to be paid at the time of the wedding and the amount of deferred *mahr* to be paid by the husband to the wife if he divorces her are agreed when the marriage is arranged and specified in the marriage contract. Jordanian law lays down that without a minimum *mahr* of one dinar, a marriage is not legal.

mukhtar   Administrative official in a village, appointed by the government to register births, land deals, and so on. The office was created by the Ottoman government in the nineteenth century as part of its drive to improve the efficiency of the administration of the empire.

sumud   Steadfastness. The political tactic of resisting the Israeli occupation by bearing all its oppressive tactics with fortitude, and refusing to leave the occupied territories in search of an easier life and better opportunities elsewhere.

ta'boun   Traditional outdoor oven for baking bread, built of mud or stone. The fuel is wood, brush or dried dung, and the flat bread is cooked on hot stones. Often several neighbouring households share a *ta'boun*, which becomes a meeting-place for women. Many Palestinian village women still bake in a *ta'boun*, although bought bread and electric ovens are increasingly available.

tawjihi   High-school graduation examinations.

thoob   Long, long-sleeved dress. The *thoob* is the traditional everyday dress of Palestinian women in the centre and south of the country, usually made of black or dark-blue fabric and embroidered with elaborate cross-stitch designs on the chest, hem and in bands up the skirt. In the past, each region had its own style and designs of embroidery, but now the designs are more universal. Many women still wear a *thoob* every day; others keep them for going out and special occasions and have simpler dresses of printed man-made fabric for everyday wear at home. Embroidering *thoobs* is one of the principal leisure activities of many village women. The man's *thoob*, a plain long robe, is still worn by a few older men, but most men, including all the younger generation, prefer Western dress. (Note: for simplicity I have used an English form of plural, *thoobs*, instead of the Arabic plural, *athwaab*.)

umm   Mother.

Map of Historical Palestine*

*Showing places mentioned in the text.
Sources: drawn by the author; outline and principal towns taken from a map provided by UNRWA (UN Refugee and Works Agency); smaller villages added by the author from an Israeli government *Survey of Israel* map, 1982.

1

The history of Palestine

The arrival of Zionism

Historical Palestine – meaning all the land now forming Israel and the West Bank and Gaza Strip, but not the Golan Heights (which are part of Syria) – was a very small area, less than four hundred kilometres from north to south, and one hundred kilometres from east to west at its widest point. From the beginning of history it was settled and ruled by a number of different peoples. The name Palestine derives from one group of early inhabitants of the coastal plain, the Philistines. Among their neighbours were the Jews, who lived and ruled with varying fortunes in the hills inland from the tenth century BC until the beginning of the Roman period. By 638 AD Palestine had been swept up in the rapid expansion of Islam; the majority of its people soon adopted the new faith and the Arabic language. In 1517 Palestine became part of the Turkish Ottoman empire, and it remained so until its capture by the British in 1917.

During most of this history, over 80 per cent of Palestinians have been Muslims belonging to the Sunni sect (which is the largest and the 'mainstream' sect in Islam world-wide). Of the many minority communities in Palestine (who have lived among the majority without the sectarian conflict endemic in modern Lebanon) the Christians were the most significant, constituting around 10 per cent of the population at the end of the Ottoman period. There was a small Jewish community continuously present from Roman times which was swelled in the eighteenth and nineteenth centuries by religious immigrants from Eastern Europe.

Under Ottoman rule, Palestine was a relatively obscure region of

1

the empire. It was poor in natural resources, with large areas of desert and arid rocky hillside; 80 per cent of its population were peasant farmers. Villages were to a great extent socially, culturally and economically self-sufficient, their contact with the government limited to tax payments through local clan heads. In the second half of the nineteenth century this picture began to change as the empire, under military and economic pressure from expansionist industrial Europe, strove to modernise itself. New land tenure laws encouraged the concentration of small farms into large estates, often owned by wealthy absentee landowners, which were farmed for profit. Peasant insecurity increased and many men left the land to find work in industries and the growing coastal port towns. At the outbreak of the First World War, a combination of high taxation, conscription, drought and locust plagues had caused severe rural poverty. Over the same period the country, which had never been politically cohesive, had become more fragmented as a result of the government's policy of concentrating power in the hands of urban notable families. The urban power-holders had little common interest or contact with their rural tenants.

Into this scenario came Zionism, the doctrine that Jews, like other nations, should have a national home for themselves. Zionism was born in the last decades of the nineteenth century in northern and eastern Europe, where Jews were facing deep-rooted anti-semitism and barbarous pogroms. In the context of the two dominant political ideas of the time, the nation-state and colonialism, the creation of their own national home seemed to some Jews an obvious response. They felt it was the only sure way Jews could protect themselves from continued persecution and discrimination. Zionism was a secular, political movement, not a religious one (and indeed was opposed for many years by much of the Judaic religious establishment), and in accordance with its pragmatic logic, various countries were proposed for the location of the 'national home'. Gradually the movement focused on Palestine, because of the unique place Palestine held in Jewish history and cultural tradition. By the time the first Zionist congress in Basle in 1897 committed itself to 'the establishment for the Jewish people of a home in Palestine secured by Public Law', nationalist-inspired Jews, mostly from Russia, had already been emigrating to Palestine for over a decade.

The new immigrants did not wish to integrate into the Palestinian population. On the contrary, their goal of transforming the land into a Jewish homeland entailed the building of a separate Jewish community with its own institutions and economic enterprises, ideally employing no Arabs and buying no Arab goods. Zionism dismissed Palestinians as primitive and unimportant. In their public pronouncements the Zionist leaders denied their ambition to establish a state and claimed that Jewish immigration would have only beneficial results for the local population; in private, however, they recognised that a national home was incompatible with the presence of a large settled population of Palestinians. The father of Zionism, Theodor Herzl, confided to his diary that Zionist settlers should 'try to spirit the penniless population across the border by procuring employment for it in the transit countries, while denying it any employment in our own (sic) country'. It quickly became clear to Palestinians that Zionism posed a danger to them, and by 1914 it was a major issue in Palestinian politics.

The Ottoman empire was defeated during the First World War, and Great Britain and France divided up its territories between them. In doing this Britain was ignoring a promise made to Arab leaders to grant them independence in exchange for assistance in the war. Meanwhile Britain had committed itself to supporting Zionism. The strategic consideration that it would be advantageous to instal a client state near the Suez Canal (to protect the vital route to India) was reinforced by ignorance of the Palestinian reality and by the presence in London of persuasive pleaders for Zionism. In the Balfour Declaration of 1917, Britain stated its readiness to help establish a national home for the Jews without prejudice to the 'rights of the existing non-Jewish communities'. To establish a Jewish home in the already fully populated land of Palestine without harming the Palestinians living there was, of course, an impossible task, as would become clear in the succeeding decades; but when Britain accepted the mandate from the League of Nations in 1922 to rule Palestine and prepare it for independence, it was with apparent disregard for the implications of the Zionist programme.

The mandatory administration was not at first unwelcome to Palestinians, and it brought them some benefits: improved health provision, road-building, agricultural training, service jobs. But although many mandate officials and some politicians in London sympathised with the Palestinian case and regularly pleaded the injustice of Zionist ambitions, the mandate was biased in favour of

Zionism. Jewish economic and institutional development was supported, but not Palestinian. Even after it had become clear that Jewish immigration was detrimental to Palestinian interests, policies to limit it were not consistently implemented. As tension built up, Jewish arms imports and military training were increasingly winked at if not officially sanctioned, whereas Palestinians were systematically deprived of arms. The imbalance was increased by the behaviour of the two communities. Whereas the growing Jewish population was determined, enterprising and highly organised, and lost no opportunity to increase its power, the Palestinians' disunity and their tactics of non-cooperation with the administration and economic boycott brought them no positive results. The British, trying to impose stability on an impossibly unstable situation, used force to punish and control both sides.

Palestinian responses and the growth of nationalism

Nationalism had been discouraged by the Ottomans, and though Arab nationalism developed in Beirut and Damascus in the late nineteenth century, this was a cultural and linguistic nationalism in response to Western cultural influence, rather than a political programme. A specifically Palestinian nationalism grew up within the boundaries determined by the mandate and in response to the threat of Zionism.

The political heritage of Palestine was not conducive to the development of a strong and well-organised national movement. The rural population was separated from the urban elite who might have led them by exploitative economic relationships, the absence of social ties, and an educational and cultural gulf. From the beginning of Zionist immigration there were popular protests against its economic results, particularly land purchase and refusal to give jobs to Arabs, but these did not develop into an organised movement until the mid 1930s. Meanwhile the urban notables were more concerned with inter-family rivalries and self-advancement than national responsibility and leadership.

In the 1930s the flood of Jewish immigrants increased dramatically as Nazism spread over Europe. The Palestinian people, driven to desperation and disillusioned with the inaction of their supposed leaders, broke into armed revolt against the British.

The first guerrilla uprising in 1935 was followed in 1936 by a general strike and further fighting in rural areas. By the time the revolt was finally suppressed in 1939, as many as five thousand Palestinians had died. The population had been thoroughly disarmed and their capacity for further resistance crushed.

The violence, however, had forced the British administration to acknowledge that the contradictions of their position were impossible to sustain and that some drastic solution had to be found. In 1937, a proposal was put forward to partition the country into two separate states, one Jewish and one Arab. When this was rejected by the leaders of the Arab community, a new suggestion was made, for a secular binational state with guaranteed Palestinian dominance. Discussions on this proposal were interrupted by the outbreak of the Second World War. The events of the next few years, especially the holocaust, made it even more unlikely than before that Zionists would accept anything less than the national state they had been working for.

During the war, the Zionists' feeling grew that Britain was not doing enough to help them. Their demands for unlimited immigration of Jews fleeing from Nazi persecution were intensified by the fact that no country in the world was willing to accept Jews in significant numbers. (The United States has been particularly accused in this respect.) The Zionist demand for a state was backed up by an escalating campaign of terrorism against the mandatory authorities. In 1947, exhausted by the war, Britain finally admitted that the situation in Palestine was uncontrollable, and announced that it would withdraw, leaving the problem to the United Nations. Under strong pressure from the United States, which had been giving wholehearted support to the Zionists for some years, the UN General Assembly voted for partition, to come into effect when Britain withdrew in May 1948.

As might have been expected, the proposed partition was not acceptable to the Palestinians or to Arab governments. Jews, who formed only 30 per cent of the population, were to be given 54 per cent of the land, of which they owned at the time only 6 per cent. The Zionist leaders accepted the plan, but it is doubtful whether they intended to accept it in the long term. The area allotted to them fell far short of their demands, and they continued to plan, train and arm themselves for seizing as much more of the land as possible. Although Israel has since claimed that it began to fight only in self-defence when Arab armies invaded after the British withdrawal in May 1948, in fact the expulsion of Palestinians began in December 1947. The first phase of the 'War of Independence' was a series of operations aimed at occupying desirable areas outside the proposed state and expelling as many Palestinians as possible. Attacks on important towns by the Zionist official army, the Haganah, were supplemented by atrocities such as the massacre by commando groups of 254 villagers at Deir Yasin in April 1948, and by other actions designed to spread terror among the population. By the time the state of Israel was declared on 15 May 1948, the day after British withdrawal, 300,000 Palestinians had already been forced to flee from their homes.

Arab resistance to the Zionist onslaught was pitiful. While Zionists had been smuggling in arms and training at least 100,000 men to fight, the Palestinian leaders and Arab governments had remained smugly blind to the danger. No serious effort was made to arm the Palestinians and prepare them to defend themselves, weakened as they were by the defeat of the 1936 revolt. The armies that the Arab states eventually sent in to try to repel the Zionist expansion were too late, too small and lacking in leadership and strategy. They were in some cases more of a hindrance than a help.

Isolated from each other, and demoralised by the impossibility of resisting without weapons, expelled villagers and townspeople started the long trek away. They carried their house-keys, expecting to return after a few weeks. With no means of transport, most could not carry any supplies to help them survive the bitter rains of winter or the heat of summer. As they left, the Zionist forces occupied or demolished their villages, and sometimes shot people who were caught returning to collect possessions from their houses or crops from their fields.

The Palestinian people scattered

When armistices were agreed in 1949, the 160,000 Palestinians who had not fled found they had become second-class and unwanted citizens of the new state of Israel, although at first they formed 25 per cent of the population. Their history will not be touched on here. Nearly five times that number, around three quarters of a million people, had been driven from their homes and sought refuge, some in the remnants of Palestine that were not under Israel's control, some in neighbouring countries. The Gaza Strip, only 45 kilometres long and 6–10 kilometres wide, with a native population of 80,000, received 190,000 refugees, becoming one of the most densely populated regions of the world and a byword for deprivation and overcrowding. Some 280,000 refugees stopped in the West Bank, where today they and their descendants form around 20 per cent of the total population. A further 100,000 fled north to Lebanon, 75,000 to Syria, and 70,000 to Jordan.[1]

The United Nations had accepted partition and recognised the new state of Israel, but did not endorse the expulsion of the Palestinian population. General Assembly resolution 194, passed in December 1948 and confirmed repeatedly since, stated that refugees must be allowed to return to their homes. But until this happened, the UN recognised its responsibility and in 1950 established the United Nations Relief and Works Agency (UNRWA) to organise camps and supply the destitute refugees' basic needs: tents, food, health care and education. As years went by, the reality of the refugees' quasi-permanent status became clear, and tents were replaced by concrete or mud-brick two-room houses. The number receiving food rations diminished as more were able to find work and support themselves, but economic possibilities for refugees have remained limited. The host countries' undeveloped economies, hardly able to support their own people, were far from having the capacity to integrate large refugee populations. (Even if it were possible, integration would have been rejected for political reasons, implying as it does the acceptance of Palestinians' permanent displacement.)

1948–67 in the West Bank and Gaza Strip

During the period 1948–67 the Gaza Strip was under Egyptian military rule, and the West Bank was annexed by Jordan. In neither case did the ruler have the resources or the interest to make significant investment in the development of the area. Politically the problem of Palestine was generally seen by Palestinians and other Arabs as the responsibility of all the Arab states. The Arab world was in a ferment of new political and economic dynamism, shaking off the heritage of colonialism and striving for a new place in the world. President Nasser of Egypt in particular adopted the Palestinian cause, hoping to unite the Arab states under his leadership. His championship was largely verbal, but many Palestinians welcomed it. Shattered by the losses and upheavals they had experienced and with all their energies absorbed by the struggle to survive, they had little choice but to wait for someone else to help them. Political activity was not dead, of course. In the Gaza Strip Nasser felt able to give limited encouragement to the growth of Palestinian militancy, but in the West Bank, expressions of Palestinian nationalism or any other destabilising dissent were quashed by the recently created Jordanian monarchy. By the 1960s Palestinians were frustrated that years of talk had brought no improvement in their situation. As a sop to their discontent rather than out of any real desire to see them independent, the Palestine Liberation Organisation (PLO) was established under the auspices of the Arab League in 1964.

It is not this date that Palestinians celebrate as most significant in their history; more important is the emergence of the guerrilla organisations. The anniversary of Fatah's first operation on 1 January 1965 is a national holiday. Fatah and other groups grew out of the realisation that instead of waiting for someone else to take action on their behalf, Palestinians must take the responsibility themselves. The failure of Nasser and other Arab states to resist Israel's invasion and occupation of the West Bank and Gaza Strip in 1967 completed Palestinians' disillusionment with Arab promises, and set the stage for the PLO. By the early 1970s an overwhelming majority of Palestinians were acknowledging the PLO as their leaders and representatives.

The Palestine Liberation Organisation

The PLO is an umbrella organisation of several groups with differing ideologies and strategies. Its 'parliament', the Palestine National Council (PNC), aims to be as representative of all sections of the Palestinian people as is possible under the circumstances. Fatah has been the dominant group within the PLO since 1969, its non-ideological nationalist programme having wide appeal. Other important groups are the Popular Front for the Liberation of Palestine (PFLP), committed to armed struggle for revolutionary change in all Arab states; and the Democratic Front for the Liberation of Palestine (DFLP), also Marxist but more willing to accept the existence of Israel. Smaller groups are variously tied to the interests of Syria, Iraq and Libya. Some of them have generally lined up with Fatah, while others have maintained hardline positions, demanding nothing less than the dissolution of the Zionist state and the restitution of the whole of Palestine. The difficulty of uniting these groups has been one reason for the slowness and caution of PLO policy development, which many international observers have found so frustrating and inexplicable.

At first military struggle was seen as the principal road to liberating Palestine: it had a heady romantic fascination for many Palestinians, recovering as they were from years of defeat and humiliation (just as it had for generations of Zionists). In the PLO's bases among the refugees in Jordan, Syria and Lebanon, military training and guerrilla operations were an important facet of its activities; so were education, health care, welfare, industrial workshops and the development of mass organisations such as trade unions and women's organisations.

After 1967 the PLO, based in Jordan, grew rapidly in membership, confidence and military strength, even though its lack of a national base and the intractability of the problem it was born to confront gave rise to many internal as well as external difficulties. In 1970–1, some elements within the PLO provoked a confrontation with the Jordanian government which led to a bloody war and the expulsion of the PLO from Jordan. The organisation moved its centre to the refugee camps in Beirut and South Lebanon. There the lack of a strong national government and the fragility of the balance between rival confessional and political groups allowed the PLO to develop considerable autonomy and freedom of action.

In the years following its establishment in Lebanon, the Palestinian movement seemed to be going from strength to strength. The 1973 war showed Israel's military might to be vulnerable, and boosted international efforts to bring the parties to a peace conference in Geneva. In 1974 the Arab League acknowledged the PLO to be the 'sole legitimate representative of the Palestinians'. The PLO leader Yaser Arafat was invited to speak to the United Nations, after which the PLO was granted observer status in the General Assembly. At the same time PLO policy was maturing. Some groups, including Fatah, were coming to believe that victory could not be achieved by military means and that the ideal goal of a state in the whole land of Palestine in which Jews and Palestinians could live together as equals was, if achievable at all, so distant as to be not worth striving for. The majority of the Palestine National Council therefore resolved to work for the establishment of a Palestinian state on as much of the land as could be liberated from Israeli rule.

The war of 1948–9 had ended with armistice agreements, not with peace, and all the Arab states continued theoretically to be in a state of war with Israel. In 1977 President Sadat reversed Egyptian policy and visited Israel, and by 1979 the Camp David agreements and a peace treaty between Egypt and Israel had been concluded. The Camp David accords were hailed internationally as a bold move which it was hoped would pave the way for peace between Israel and all its other neighbours and the resolution of the Palestinian problem. But although Palestinians in the occupied territories are the principal subject of the Camp David agreement, they were neither consulted when the proposals were drawn up nor invited to give their approval. In fact, the Camp David proposals were and still are fundamentally unacceptable to Palestinians. Far from recognising the Palestinians as a nation with a right like any other to self-determination, the accords propose an ill-defined Palestinian control over a limited range of local affairs in parts of the occupied territories – called 'autonomy' – while leaving Israel with overall power. They make no reference to the PLO as the Palestinians' representative, and very little to wider questions of Palestinian rights.

While the world was hailing the Camp David protagonists Prime Minister Begin, President Sadat and US President Carter as historic peace-makers, from the Palestinians' point of view Camp David was a blow against peace and justice rather than a step towards them. With Egypt prevented by the peace treaty from intervening, Israel was free to deal with other opponents, and began to do so immediately by launching an attack on Lebanon in 1978. This was aimed at destroying the PLO and imposing Israeli control on South Lebanon. It was followed by further attacks culminating in the 1982 invasion, the PLO's expulsion from Beirut, and the massacre in the Sabra and Shatila refugee camps.

Between 1982 and the beginning of the *intifada* in 1987, the PLO suffered its most difficult and dispiriting period. With no secure location, and with its military strength, such as it was, destroyed, it struggled to maintain its independence and develop new strategies. It received no real support either from Syria, whose interest was to gain control over it, or from Jordan, which until July 1988 always intended to retain its own sovereignty over any Palestinian entity that might come into existence in the West Bank. Tense relations with the Arab states were reflected in violent splits within the PLO itself, brought to an end largely by the Syrian attacks on the refugee camps in Lebanon in 1987. During this period the USA and Israel remained adamant in their refusal to accept the PLO as a negotiating partner, maintaining that the PLO did not represent the majority of Palestinians and was committed to terrorism and the destruction of Israel.

During these two decades, one and a quarter million Palestinians have been living in the occupied territories, sometimes in the news and sometimes out, sometimes having a significant shaping influence on PLO thinking, sometimes not.

Life under occupation

First-time visitors are sometimes puzzled by the signs of apparent prosperity, especially in the West Bank: lavish new villas lining the roads, televisions and cassette players in the simplest homes. But poverty underlies the occasional glitter. The standard of housing and amenities is very low in villages and camps, and public services are inadequate. Palestinians do not enjoy the protection of welfare services, unemployment benefit, sick pay or insurance. The comforts of urban consumerism where they do exist have often been bought at a high price – work for long hours in humiliating conditions in Israel, or emigration to the Gulf or North or South America. And the villas may have been built because opportunities for investing hard-earned wealth more productively in agriculture or industry are so limited. In any case, material standard of living is not the only criterion of a just and dignified existence. Israeli and US-backed schemes to 'improve the quality of life', touted as a solution to the problem of occupation in the mid-1980s, were a distraction from the real issue, which was Palestinians' lack of freedom and the denial of their rights to control and organise life for themselves.

Palestinians under occupation have no representation, no freedom of expression or association, no economic activity without permit, no absolute right to move around or even to live in their own country. While these restrictions are felt more by the politically active and in some exposed professions than by isolated farmers or housewives, everyone is affected by the absence of individual dignity and privacy, the harassment and humiliation experienced in every encounter with administrative authority, the military or settlers. Everyone too feels fear – fear of attack by settlers, fear that a member of the family might be arrested and probably ill-treated (it has been said that three-quarters of all families in the occupied territories have lost a family member to prison at some time), fear of the army's arbitrary powers to impose curfew, seal and demolish houses, or close business premises.[2] Rights of appeal exist in theory but in practice are negligible. A fair trial might be held in a purely civil or domestic matter, but in anything which touches the needs of the occupation is out of the question. Women bear the burden of bringing up families and running homes in the absence of state support and services. The restrictions men place on their freedom of movement are often increased as the presence of the Israeli military creates a permanent sense of insecurity, fear and violation.

Law and the administration of occupation

In the immediate aftermath of its victory in June 1967, Israel was not certain what to do with the territories it had occupied. They could have been returned to their previous rulers in exchange for political and military concessions, but there were various arguments for retaining possession of them. Most Israelis felt that Israeli control of the occupied territories was essential for their country's security. There was the religious-expansionist view, also held to some extent by many non-religious Israelis (who formed three-quarters of the population), that God had promised to the Jewish people the whole of the land between the Jordan and the Mediterranean. The desire to control vital water resources, located in the hills of the West Bank and Golan Heights, was also a consideration, and soon the economic benefits of continuing occupation began to play a significant role. The territories offered a pool of cheap labour for Israeli industries and a sizeable captive market for Israeli goods.

The moment for an early political settlement passed, and most Israelis grew accustomed to the idea that the occupied territories were rightfully part of Israel, although it was not clear what their legal status should be. International law exists to regulate temporary military occupation during war, but it does not countenance prolonged or permanent occupation. Annexation – full incorporation of the occupied land legally and politically into the occupying power – is specifically illegal. Israel did nonetheless annex East Jerusalem, to which it felt its cultural and historical ties were irrefutable. For most Israelis annexation of the rest of the territories was not an option. The *raison d'être* of Israel is that it is a Jewish state, and annexation would force a choice between two equally unacceptable courses. Either Palestinians living in the West Bank and Gaza Strip would be given full citizenship rights, in which case the total population of the enlarged state would be nearly half Palestinian; or they would be given less than full citizenship under an *apartheid*-like system, which would be incompatible with Israel's commitment to democracy.

In the absence of a permanent answer, the illegal prolongation of military occupation – rule by force – emerged as the most advantageous solution. The ambiguous situation of the territories remained as a moral and political problem for Israel that would have to solved. By virtue of its superior force and good international public relations, Israel was able to shelve the question for twenty years, but the *intifada* forced the future of the territories into the forefront of the political agenda. Israelis had to face the truth: force is not a viable long-term method of ruling an unwilling population of two million, and compromises the moral and democratic claims of the Jewish state.

Many of the institutions in the West Bank and Gaza Strip such as schools and hospitals, and the machinery of administration and law, were inherited from previous rulers. Palestinians form the bulk of employees and pay for these institutions themselves through taxation, but the appearance of self-rule is specious, as each sphere is under the direct authority of the military government. Pre-existing law has been adapted by well over a thousand military orders, almost every activity is subject to specific permit, and all adults have to carry identity cards which are a much-used tool of control and harassment. Security arguments and 'emergency' powers enable the authorities on many occasions to by-pass legal processes and rule through direct military intervention. They have powers of search, arrest and detention, deportation, collective punishments such as curfews, travel bans and house demolitions, confiscation of land and property, censorship and closure of organisations. As was tragically clear during the *intifada*, accepted methods of crowd control include heavy use of tear-gas and shooting to kill. Palestinians for most of the period of the occupation have had no political rights at all, and membership of the PLO is illegal and severely punished.

'Creating facts': trying to make occupation irreversible

Because Israel's aim is somehow to incorporate the occupied territories into Israel, control by force is not enough. Various means have been tried to implant Israeli presence and make it irreversible and acceptable to the Palestinians. One brutally simple tactic is to reduce the number of Palestinians living in the territories. Any Palestinian who was outside at the time of the 1967 invasion was not allowed to return except at the Israeli authorities' discretion after a long and difficult appeal process. Even today, those who leave to work or study have to cope with many restrictions on their right to return. Though 'transfer' of the population out of the country has only emerged into public discussion in the late 1980s, the policy from the beginning has been to make life difficult and uncomfortable so that as many Palestinians as possible decide to leave 'voluntarily'.

The standard of living has been undermined by restrictions on the development of public services and amenities, either by direct control or by under-resourcing. The economic growth of the occupied territories has been deliberately stifled, with military orders and the power of permit-issue being used to control development in agriculture, industry, and house-building. Arbitrary and punitive tax assessments are used to try to force merchants and manufacturers out of business. As well as pushing people to leave in search of work and opportunity, this policy of economic pressure has served a second long-term purpose, creating Palestinian dependence on Israel for jobs and goods – food, industrial and consumer goods.

Another approach to permanent implantation has been the drive to establish a Jewish population in settlements at strategic points in the occupied territories. This was a central policy from the mid 1970s, and one that has aroused particularly strong feelings in Palestinians and in international opinion. Half the land in the West Bank and Gaza Strip has been possessed by various means – quasi-legal or illegal according to international law – for the building of settlements. Settlers are supported by a conspicuously superior infrastructure and have many economic and legal privileges, such as the right to bear arms.

Any oppressing power has to try to control political ideas and leadership, and the Israeli authorities have been no exception. Political groups and meetings are illegal in the occupied territories; the censorship and banning of books and newspapers are strict; and most organisations and cultural institutions have suffered interference or temporary or permanent closure. Tight control is exercised over curricula, materials and teachers in schools. Individuals who are active or prominent in public life are threatened, harassed, intimidated, imprisoned and sometimes deported.

Many of Israel's specific policies and measures, as well as its ultimate purpose of making permanent its control over the occupied territories, are contrary to international agreements and laws. The Geneva Conventions on the protection of civilians under occupation forbid in general the intervention of the occupier in non-security matters, so all Israeli interference in economic life, education or control of water use, for instance, violates the Conventions. The confiscation of land, the transfer of population from the occupying power into the occupied territories, and new taxation of the occupied population are specifically forbidden. In security matters, too, Israel violates the minimum rules, for instance in its treatment of prisoners. Israel is a signatory to the Geneva Conventions but argues that they do not apply to the case of the Palestinian territories, because these were not self-governing states before they were occupied. (This argument is not accepted by most of the other signatory states.)

Resistance to occupation

From the first days of occupation in June 1967 until the 1987 *intifada* Palestinians were not able to mount any sustained, concerted resistance. The possibilities of military resistance under occupation were extremely limited, as the small size of the country and the thoroughness of Israeli surveillance made it impossible to amass arms or train on any significant scale. Only in the refugee camps of the Gaza Strip were guerrillas able to pose a real threat to Israeli control, until they were crushed by General Ariel Sharon in 1971. As long as armed struggle was a key part of PLO strategy, all the main PLO factions supplemented their military activities outside by developing military cells in the territories and undertook occasional operations. These were immensely important for Palestinian morale, proving the vulnerability of Israel and the unquenchability of Palestinian spirit, but their practical effects were probably only to increase the vigilance of the Israeli military and the fears and hostility of the Israeli public.

Attachment to the military option, combined with the lack of experienced leaders and organisations and the harshness of Israeli military rule, prevented Palestinians from developing far in the direction of active non-violent resistance. It was not that there was any question, for the vast majority, of accepting the occupation. For some the first choice was to attempt to negotiate with Israel a return of the territories to the previous status quo – government by Jordan and Egypt. When this came to nothing, and as the PLO gained strength outside, more and more Palestinians in the occupied territories chose the course of waiting for the PLO to win their liberation. Their own role was to refuse to legitimate the occupation by accepting it, and to use non-co-operation and non-violent demonstrations to draw world attention to its most blatant violations of legality and acceptability. In some cases, non-violent resistance did succeed in reversing particular policies of the occupation: one example is the refusal of schools in East Jerusalem (the Palestinian side of Jerusalem) to accept the imposition of an Israeli curriculum after the annexation of East Jerusalem.

The unquestionable achievement of Palestinian resistance is that after twenty years of occupation, Palestinians in the occupied territories have not given up: far from lapsing into despair and accepting the Israeli view of the world, their sense of national identity and strength and their belief in their rights and eventual victory are stronger than before, and shared by more individuals and nations of the world. This is the result of a method of resistance that every individual in the occupied territories has been able to participate in. The proud determination to bear suffering and humiliation and not be forced into exile or submission is a mode of resistance that the people of the occupied territories, with so few possibilities of positive action, made particularly their own and gave a name to: *sumud* – steadfastness. Since the aim of Israel is to deny and to end the existence of the Palestinians as a people in their own country, it is an act of resistance in itself to continue assertively to exist, to stay put and not to give in.

In the mid 1970s, Palestinians outside and in the occupied territories realised that endurance and occasional bursts of resistance were not enough. If the occupation was to continue for years, it was important to develop the people politically. They must be educated and activated, their unity strengthened beyond a mere shared emotion into organisation, and structures established which could be the basis for self-reliance. Mass organisations came into being with the aims of developing the community socially and politically. These included youth organisations for voluntary work on harvests, road-building and village improvement, as well as cultural and educational activities; professional associations and trade unions to work for improved rights and conditions and to provide services to members; and voluntary medical groups. Educational institutions were expanded, cultural and intellectual life flourished, and long-term national strategies for social and economic development began to be debated. It was in this period that the mass women's organisations were founded which will form the subject of a later chapter in this book.

At the same time, the occupied territories were developing a new political strength and contributing their own voice to the dialogue within the PLO. In the municipal elections which Israel allowed in the West Bank in 1976, candidates who supported the PLO swept the board, giving a new confidence and confirming the emergence of a new leadership in the territories. When the Camp David accords were signed setting out a 'peace process' on Israeli terms, it was the people of the occupied territories, not the PLO leadership outside, who erupted into protest and made it clear to the world that Palestinians were not ready to concede defeat. The occupied territories had become a political force in their own right. It came as no surprise that the dramatic reversals of world opinion towards the PLO in 1988 were sparked off not by the cautious diplomacy of the PLO leadership but by the *intifada* which had begun in the Gaza Strip.

Women

Throughout the history of Palestine in the twentieth century, women have played a much more active part than conventional European images of submissive Arab women would attribute to them. They experienced much suffering and were often helpless victims, and many were no doubt trapped in the silence and domestic preoccupation characteristic of their subordinate social position. On the other hand many individuals gave active support to men in their struggles. Some took up arms themselves. Many groups of women organised to press for social change and political progress and to help victims survive; many women emerged as leaders with new ideas and ambitions for the Palestinian people. In the following chapters women tell how they experienced and contributed to this history. They have dealt with wars and upheavals, personal losses and exile, and with social, educational and economic changes that would have spanned several generations in Europe. My oldest informant was married at the age of seven to protect her from Turkish soldiers during the First World War. As a refugee, she took part in demonstrations against the Jordanian government in the 1950s, and is now proud of her grandchildren, some of whom are in and out of prison for their student political activities, while others are working as doctors and engineers in Eastern Europe and waiting for their opportunity to come home. The youngest woman who appears here is a seventeen-year-old student at a vocational training college, who has chosen Islam as her framework and support in her campaign to liberate the thinking and the social life of women in her village. They are very different women, whose lives and interests hardly overlap, but they represent some of the currents and developments in Palestinian life of the mid 1980s – currents that they hope will be fulfilled in a very different future.

2

Women's position in traditional society

Palestine's location at the eastern end of the Mediterranean puts it at a historical meeting-point of different cultural and political forces: two religions, Christianity and Islam (three, of course, but Judaism had little impact on Palestinian society before 1948); two cultures, Mediterranean and Arab; two types of economy, settled agriculture and the nomadic pastoralism of the Arabian deserts. Northern Europeans tended, for reasons of historical rivalry, to think of Muslim and Christian, Ottoman and European, as polarities, essentially different; in Palestine these poles met and complemented each other. European travellers may have been most struck by those elements in Palestinian society that confirmed their image of 'the exotic orient', but in reality Palestine's was predominantly a peasant agricultural society sharing many characteristics with other peasant cultures, particularly those around the Mediterranean. In both Bedu and settled communities, the mechanism that arose for controlling wealth – whether herds or land or both – was the patrilineal family. The subordinate position of women, which Europeans have sometimes thought of as particularly Islamic, is in fact imposed by the institution of the patriarchal family and is equally characteristic of most other cultures, including that of Europe. There are still many similarities between the life of women in rural Portugal or Greece and the life of Syrian or Palestinian peasant women. A generation ago the parallels would have been clearer. The lives of women, both Muslim and Christian, were framed in a similar ideology of family, honour and chastity.

Throughout this chapter I will use for convenience the past tense to describe Palestine's traditional society. I do not mean to suggest that the traditional social structures and relationships have passed into history. As will become clear, Palestinian women of today grow up within a framework of ideals and restrictions which, although relaxed since their mothers' and grandmothers' days, has not fundamentally changed.

The structure of rural society

Two interlocking structures claimed the loyalty of rural Palestinians, the village and the *hamouleh* (often translated as tribe or clan, though there is no exactly equivalent word in English). This was at least the ideological framework of society. If as an account of reality it is a simplification, this does not alter the fact that Palestinians lived and conceptualised their lives not primarily as individuals but as parts of a family group. The structure shaped men's lives as much as women's, but women collectively had lower status than men, and it is women's particular relationship of dependence within the group that concerns us here.

A *hamouleh* was a group of extended families claiming descent from a common ancestor. Some *hamayel* (plural) were large, spreading over several villages in a region; many were smaller, forming part of the population of one village. Within one *hamouleh*, families could occupy very different economic and social positions. A *hamouleh* could hold land communally and operated as a collectivity, dominated by authoritarian patriarchs. The patriarchal structure was repeated at lower levels, in the extended families that made up the *hamouleh*, and in the component households of the families. Each household was responsible for its own internal affairs, while over all the member families extended the authority of the *hamouleh* elders when questions arose which touched the wealth or honour of the whole *hamouleh*. At every level the interests of individuals were subordinated to the interests of the group. Before capitalist economic relations and the modern state had developed their controls over so many aspects of civic life, the *hamouleh* fulfilled many functions: the accumulation and distribution of resources, the protection and support of individuals, and the maintenance of law and order.

Women were more enclosed within the family than men, their movements and their economic contribution being largely restricted to the domestic sphere. Their participation in non-domestic affairs when it occurred was indirect and not publicly recognised, and at no stage of their lives were they expected to be independent. Women's principal function was to bear sons through whom the family's wealth and strength would be perpetuated. This function is still honoured in the usual form of address to a married woman, *Umm* ('Mother of') followed by the name of her eldest son. (The primacy of reproduction over other activities is revealed in the fact that men are addressed in the same way, as *Abu*, 'Father of' their son). The Arabic language itself reflects a tendency to think of women in terms of their role as wives. They belong to one of two categories – marriageable, or already married: one word, *bint*, serves for girl, daughter, virgin, and unmarried woman.

Patrilineal families can only be reproduced through the birth of sons of undoubted paternity, so marriage, as the mechanism for restricting a woman to sexual relations with one man, is essential. There was great pressure on both men and women to marry. The need for marriage was justified, in Islamic text and commentary and in popular belief, by various moral and biological explanations. Sexuality, while held to be natural and impossible to suppress, was thought dangerous and wicked if not channelled into marital relationships. Women were thought to be weak and unable to survive without the protection and material support that men provided in exchange for women's work as wives. Women who managed to live on their own challenged this view, so it was unacceptable for them to do so, and the social system tried to preclude the necessity. There is a tension inherent in patrilineal social systems between a woman's ties to her natal family and to her marital family; the continued responsiblity of her father's family protected a woman against ill-treatment by her husband's, and sometimes allowed her some space to make choices. But she was expected to be dependent on one or the other throughout her life. If her husband died she would remain with his family; if he divorced her or for some other reason failed as a protector, she would return to the charge of her own father, uncles or brothers. It was common in village custom for a woman to seal her dependence on her brothers by handing back to them any land she inherited from her parents, often in exchange for a share of the produce.

Honour

Hamayel achieved status in relation to one another not so much through wealth, size and power as by the maintenance of honour. The honour code may have been inherited by the Arab people from the desert tribes of the pre-Islamic period, but it is also found in other, non-Arab societies, especially around the Mediterranean. In Palestinian peasant society there were components of honour that the Homeric Greeks would have recognised – courage, generosity, magnanimity. Honour also related to land and to qualities associated with land: stability and long history, plentiful sons, good husbandry. *'Ma illu ard, fish 'indu 'ard'* – 'He who has no land, has no honour' – is a saying that has gained poignancy since the Palestinian people lost most of their land to Israel.

Honour was not a measure of individual moral qualities; it pertained to families, not individuals, and was a relationship between a family and the community. The essential was what the community saw when it looked at the family, what it said about it and how it behaved towards it. One salient requirement of honour in conservative peasant communities was the willingness to conform with the community's customs. Every family had its honour and strove to maintain it, irrespective, to some extent, of wealth, personal morality or 'justice' in any abstract sense. Questions of honour were not judged according to Western moral standards of absolute right and wrong. In vengeance as in reconciliation, both parties to a dispute had the right and the duty to defend their honour.

Honour was measured and sustained in a very literal way. Insults to a family's honour had to be avenged in kind or in material compensation. If a man was killed, any member of his family, all of whom were accountable for the family's honour, had to avenge the death by killing a member of the offending family; they in turn had to redeem their honour by killing another of the injured family, and the process of reciprocal vengeance could continue, sometimes for years, until both parties called a halt and a formal public reconciliation was made, which preserved the honour of both.

One function of the ideology of honour was to support the internal structure of the family; to be precise, to idealise men's control over women. Its most keenly felt daily requirement was that the male members of a family should protect the female from all dangers, but particularly from sexual impurity. The supremacy of this demand over other aspects of honour was demonstrated in 1948, when many of the Palestinian families who fled their homes did so primarily out of fear that their women would be raped by Zionist soldiers. This was an old fear, but one that the Zionists, apparently through careful preparatory study of Palestinian society, had realised was still potent. For many Palestinian men, saving their women from rape was more important than defending their homes or showing personal bravery and defiance. This Achilles' heel of national resistance was subsequently acknowledged and condemned in a reversal of the old saying:*'Al-ard qabil al-'ard'* – 'Land before Honour'.

The relationship between a society's ideal of honour, its perception of women and the requirement of sexual modesty, is a subject of debate among anthropologists. Various explanations have been suggested for the origins and idealised justifications of the code. For the moment, it is enough to say that honour was a family and *hamouleh* value, and therefore a male value because it was through its men that a family related with the wider world. The ideal of honour, therefore, was made up of qualities which were seen as masculine. It was men who actively had to seek and defend honour, while women were to some degree passive objects in the system. This duality reinforced the duality of gender ideals: the more men saw themselves as protectors, the more women had to be seen as needing protection. There was a constant ideological pressure to keep women as helpless and dependent as possible. They had to be perceived as weak, less intelligent, emotional, lacking self-control, amoral, unable to defend their families' honour or deal with the harshness and complexities of the world outside the home. In other words, an idea of the 'feminine' was imposed on women that was very similar to that familiar to Europeans and Americans.

A woman's main contribution to her family's honour was the indisputable reputation for sexual purity: a passive enough achievement, but even this men did not allow women to win entirely through their own efforts. Women were expected to behave modestly, but it was men who ensured women's chastity by keeping them covered up and out of sight as much as possible. This practice contained its own reinforcement, for in a society accustomed to the seclusion of women within their families, when a woman went out alone or mixed with non-family men, it would be assumed she was 'up to no good'. Men had to be extreme in their restrictiveness if they were to protect their family's honour against slander.

Constant vigilance about chastity generated obsession with its fragility and fear of the power of sexuality. It was a small step from the thought that a woman could not be trusted to manage her own sexuality to the idea that women were responsible for all violations of sexual propriety. It was the victim who was blamed in cases of rape, and sometimes a woman suspected of an illicit sexual contact would be sacrificed to preserve her family's honour.

Seclusion

Murder was the extreme form of victimisation. Seclusion and the resulting mental deprivation, on the other hand, were women's everyday experiences. From puberty onwards (often put at around nine years old, to be on the safe side) girls were separated from all men except those of the 'forbidden degrees' – that is, men so closely related that they would not be allowed to marry them (brothers, father, uncles). Young women had to spend most of their time at home, keeping to a separate room when male visitors were received. Preferably they would go outside only in company with other girls, and not leave the immediate area of the home except under the protection of a man. Total seclusion was not possible, as peasant houses were not large enough to have separate quarters for women. Besides, women had to work in the fields, collect water and firewood, tend animals, and visit relatives in pursuance of many social and practical duties. Palestinian rural women never wore veils; veiling was a status symbol of the urban upper classes. For ordinary women modesty was preserved by wearing ankle-length, long-sleeved dresses and keeping their heads covered when they were outside. In addition, women were required to behave modestly, walking with lowered eyes, not speaking to people in the street, and being quiet and unassertive in conversation. The restrictions were applied most strictly to unmarried girls, and the extra difficulty of protecting the reputations of young virgins was probably a factor, along with the desire for large numbers of children, in the early marriage that was common in at least some periods of Palestinian history. Older women, deemed past the age of sexual activity, might be allowed a little more freedom in mixing with men, but this was not always the case.

The effects of seclusion on women's lives were far-reaching. Lack of education and lack of participation in public life kept women dependent on men intellectually. Though they were legally entitled to their own property, custom encouraged women to be economically dependent too, restricting them to working on their husband's land.

Women's freedom was limited, but they had their own domain and respected place in a viable social system, so their acceptance of their limited role should not be interpreted as being simply the result of force. The system could not have survived so long if the sexes had been in a perpetual state of war. As they grew up, learning their society's ideals and expectations, women internalised the honour system as much as men did. They strove to achieve honour themselves as far as this lay within their scope, and mostly fulfilled their marital and maternal duties uncomplainingly. When women suffered individually from paternal tyranny or marital cruelty, they saw their sufferings as individual and natural occurrences, not as products of a social organisation that was inherently oppressive.

Community responsibility

The honour of families and especially the virtue of their women were accepted as being the responsibility of the whole community. Not just family members but anyone in the village or neighbourhood had the right to report violations of propriety to the woman's father or husband. Neighbours were constantly on the watch to see who went where and why. If a girl was seen talking to a man, her father would soon hear about it and he would not consider the neighbour who reported it to him an interfering busybody. She was doing him a service, helping him to maintain the honour of his family and the effective functioning of the system. Since honour was a matter of external appearance, it had to be constantly open to inspection and to be proved by contact with the external environment. Honour consisted precisely of what other people said, so no family could risk any non-conformity with the most conservative of norms. The slightest deviation would arouse comment which would be, in itself, dishonour.

The mutual concern for honour was the community's way of working together to maintain itself and protect itself from disintegration; its obverse side could be competitiveness and malice. It was all too easy to harm a neighbour's status by impugning his honour with gossip about his family. The fear that a woman's neighbours were watching eagerly for the slightest excuse to topple her family from their honoured position was a pervasive and unchallengeable constraint on her behaviour.

Women in Islam

Muslims believe that the *Koran* (or *Quran*), being the Word of God, is absolute and complete; to a non-Muslim it appears to contain as much that is contradictory, ambiguous or open to different interpretations as any other scripture. It is not possible to state definitively 'what Islam says about women'. Some verses of the *Koran* urge that women should be treated as men's equals, while others explicitly state their inferiority. The contradictions probably arose from tensions and contradictions in the changing society in which the Prophet Mohammed lived and taught. Scholars have different views of exactly what these forces were and how they related to the rise of Islam, but there is wide agreement on one point. Women in the period before Islam appear to have had very low status, being treated as little better than commodities. Mohammed could not change this attitude altogether, but he improved women's position in many ways, establishing for them some statutory rights and insisting on their equal humanity.

The women who appear by name in the *Koran* and the early history of Islam were individuals, autonomous in their thoughts and actions, proud, sharp-witted, and confident enough to debate and argue with the Prophet. They were not condemned for being so. Indeed, Mohammed's respect for his young wife Aisha was so great that he advised his followers to learn half their religion from her. Islam established women's right to economic independence, stating clearly that they can own and inherit property and run their own businesses. It asserted that in legal matters women are responsible individuals, giving them the right to bring legal cases without the consent of their husbands, and to be the legal guardians of minors. It limited polygyny and restricted men's rights to divorce by instituting a three-month waiting period and insisting that divorce is 'hateful to Allah'.

All this was certainly progress and gave women greater legal status than they had in Europe until very recently. On the other hand, apologists for Islam cannot ignore the fact that although women were granted equality to men in the sight of Allah, they were not given equality to men in the world. Islamic society was still patriarchal, and the concomitant superiority of men was roundly affirmed:

> Men have authority over women because Allah has made the one superior to the other, and because they spend their wealth to maintain them. Good women are obedient. They guard their unseen parts because Allah has guarded them. As for those from whom you fear disobedience, admonish them and send them to beds apart and beat them. Then if they obey you, take no further action against them. Allah is high, supreme.[1]

Though in some respects Islam did give women positive rights, in the matter of sexual relations, which is the basis of their social position and power, it gave them almost none. Polygyny was permitted, although not encouraged. A woman was to be available at the pleasure of her husband, for his use, and for him only: 'Women are your fields: go, then, into your fields as you please'.[2]

Women's inferior status was made explicit and legal, while the kindness that might mitigate it was left a matter of individual conscience. The *Koran* may be a charter of women's rights, but not of their equal rights; Islamic societies as they have developed since the Prophet's time have not been reluctant to exploit all the possibilities of domination that the law allows them, while they have ignored the Prophet's exhortations to treat women as equals. Inequality has suited their practical needs better. The *Koran*, asserting as it does women's biological, intellectual, social, economic and legal inferiority, is understood as the divine endorsement of the patriarchal tribal and peasant social systems.

The course of women's lives

A girl was greeted at birth as a more or less unwelcome addition to the family. Once she was married, her work and her child-bearing capacity would contribute to the strength of the family she married into, not her father's, and it was sons, not daughters, who supported parents in their old age. (There is no evidence that female infanticide was practised in Palestine, but even today statistics of infant mortality and morbidity can be interpreted as suggesting that girl babies are often, as elsewhere, victims of deliberate or unconscious neglect.)

The age of marriage varied. In the early decades of this century it appears to have been common for girls to wait until after twenty; then, with an improvement in the economic situation, the age dropped. Most of the older women I spoke to had been married at the age of thirteen or fourteen, but now expectations have changed and they disapprove of such an early start to adulthood. Umm Fawwaz, a rural woman married in about 1942:

> I'm ashamed to tell you how young I was when I married – four months short of fourteen. I hadn't started my periods, I was skinny and flat-chested, nothing up there at all.

Another village woman Umm Jihad, married in 1955, felt she had been luckier:

> My sister Miriam was only twelve when she was married. She was so immature that her husband left her at home with her mother for a year afterwards. He treated her like a baby, bringing her nuts and melon-seeds when he came to visit. My father saw that she was unhappy, and decided not to marry me until I was eighteen – unusually old at that time. I was much better prepared.

Marriage was arranged by parents – the mother often being responsible for finding a suitable spouse – with the object of making a new alliance or consolidating the family. Palestinians preferred marriage within the family. Marriage was not necessarily a very strong bond; in Islam it is a contract, not a sacrament as it is in Christianity, and it can easily be dissolved. Blood relationship was stronger, so marriage within the family was a stronger bond than marriage outside. Other points in its favour were that a woman was less likely to be ill-treated by her own kin than by strangers, and that it did not entail a transfer of wealth outside the family. The ideal marriage was between the son of one brother and the daughter of another. This was not actually very common, but an eligible cousin would be offered first refusal of a girl before any other candidate was approached.

Among the older women I met, the traditional marriage by arrangement was still seen as having more likelihood of success than a random alliance between unknown families. Even though her married life was disastrous, 55-year-old Umm Suleiman expressed no regrets about how it began:

> I knew my husband a little; we were cousins. Our families had always gone down to the land together in the spring and lived side by side, so I knew them well and they were good people.

Unless the betrothed couple were close relations, they would quite probably never have met each other, and in any case they were not supposed to see each other during the period of their engagement; 65-year-old Umm Issa laughed as she remembered the time of her marriage:

> I was married when I was twelve. Do you think we knew each other like couples do today? Not at all! Your father chose you a husband, and if you didn't like him your father would beat you and force you to accept him. We weren't like the girls of today, who make all their own decisions. If a girl refused to marry the man her father chose for her, we used to say, 'May Allah put her eyes out'.

Umm Issa's is a harsh view of the past. Actual levels of violence against women, past or present, would be as hard to discover in Palestine as anywhere else. But coercion need not require force. Parents' economic and psychological power over their daughter was strong, and her legal right to withhold her consent to a marriage would mean little in practice. She might not even be present at her own marriage, her father representing her instead.

Bride-price – *mahr*

Among Muslims an important element in marriage negotiations was fixing the *mahr* or dower, to be paid by the groom to the family of the bride. (Christians did not pay *mahr*, and they regarded this as a sign of the moral superiority they sometimes claimed over Muslims.) The size of the *mahr* varied from region to region and through time, depending on the general level of disposable wealth.

Each community had its own standard, around which the amount in individual cases varied according to factors such as the closeness of the relationship between the two families, or the extent of their obligation to each other. It was paid to the father, who passed some of it on to his daughter as her own inalienable wealth to support her through the possible vicissitudes of married life. It often took the form of gold coins for her to wear in her headdress, and perhaps some clothes and household goods. The groom also gave gifts to the bride, and as part of the marriage contract he had to promise a further sum to be paid to her in the event of divorcing her. (If the wife herself sought divorce, she forfeited this 'deferred *mahr*'.)

Umm Issa explained how the *mahr* was calculated and paid in her village, which at the time of her marriage in the early 1930s was unusually poor and isolated from Palestine's increasingly money-using economy:

> My father had two men offering for my hand. One was a close cousin, the other a more distant one, but he had worked for my father on his land for seven years, so my father chose him. Because of the rivalry, my *mahr* was higher than usual – I was worth thirty dinars instead of the usual twenty-five. People hardly had any money in those days, so the *mahr* was usually paid in wheat or barley. Doesn't that make you laugh? My cousins were all paid for in barley. Mine was in money, but I don't know where it went. Our fathers swallowed all our *mahr* up themselves. All my father gave me was one mattress and one quilt; and I had two more mattresses and quilts and one dress from my husband. I didn't have any gold; my husband was an orphan and very poor.

Umm Jihad, ten years younger and from a richer region, was part of an exchange marriage, a bargain in which brides were exchanged between families. Her regret that she did not receive any *mahr* reveals how women viewed the payment: it was both a security for their future, to which they were legally entitled, and a sign of the respect in which they were held.

> My brother married a girl from the next village, and her brother asked for me. My sisters had been given 130 dinars each when they married; our father kept 100 and gave them the rest to buy gold coins. But because mine was an exchange marriage, our families reached an agreement that neither side would pay anything. It was a shameful thing to do to me, and dangerous too. A woman needs some money of her own. People say, 'Never mind, her husband can buy her some gold later', but it never works out like that. Once you have children, where's the extra money going to come from?

A wedding was, as it is everywhere, an occasion for communal celebration and for displays of wealth and generosity. Days of feasting, music and dancing, in which the whole village might share, culminated in a procession carrying the bride to her husband's home. Some young brides enjoyed the only moment of importance they had known in their lives. Umm Hatem, from a prominent family in the town of Hebron:

> I was only thirteen and had never seen my husband, but I didn't know anything to be unhappy about. I was happy and singing because of the new clothes I got. That's how it was then.

Umm Fawwaz:

> It was exciting to be getting new clothes, and my first pair of shoes. It was something to be dressed up like a queen and have everyone looking at me as I rode the horse away from my father's house.

If it was her first marriage, the honour of both families required that the bride's virginity be proved, so defloration was a fairly public event. In some villages, I was told, the male guests used to watch through the windows and shout encouragement to the new husband. (Some women told me, with great scorn and disapproval, that this still happens in remote villages, but I never heard first-hand evidence of it.) Proof was more often offered in the form of a display of the blood-stained sheet or shift. First experiences of sex were not happy, I was told. Umm Fawwaz blamed her parents for most of the sufferings of her unhappily married life, including this one:

> My mother wasn't very clever, she hadn't told me anything. I didn't know how to have babies, I didn't even know that a man has to sleep with his wife. I don't think my husband did either, he was only eighteen.

Umm Hatem:

> When my husband first got into bed with me, I was so astonished, I fought him. He hit me and knocked me out of bed – I've still got the scar!

Umm Fawwaz was no better prepared for the other duties of married life:

My mother hadn't taught me anything. I was living like a sheep, just eating, if you want to know the truth. My older sisters knew how to cook and make bread, but I'd just had the duties of a younger sister, going down to our land and bringing back figs and things.

But a young wife, living as a junior member in a household ruled by her mother-in-law, had time to learn. Everybody's servant at first, her position would improve when she proved her worth by bearing sons. If she was so unfortunate as to be childless (and bearing only daughters was not much better) her low status would last all her life. Sons were the focus of a woman's life, justification of her existence, and her emotional centre in a situation where relationships between husband and wife were not necessarily close. Umm Fawwaz lived through twelve years of childless marriage, often alone with her parents-in-law because her husband, an only child, was in America. She described how she felt when her first child was born:

I was so happy. Everybody said I was just imagining I was pregnant, but I knew they were wrong. I didn't go to my mother for help, nor to my mother-in-law – they'd done little enough for me. I gave all my time to my son. I even paid a woman to come and wash and clean for me so that I could care for him all the time. I was so afraid for him, I didn't like anyone else to kiss him. Every evening after I'd put him to bed, I sat listening and watching, I wouldn't even let a mosquito get near him, I was quite peaceful, contented and comfortable for a while after he was born.

For Umm Hatem, happy memories were overlaid with exhaustion and worry:

I started having babies – three girls first. People criticised me and I was ashamed, although my husband loved them. Then I had sons – eight of them. All my life I haven't had time to think about anything except my children – thirty years of it. I had thirteen, I must have been mad.

Birth-control, though known in medieval times (the great Islamic scholar Al Ghazali, for example, wrote a treatise on it) was little known and suspect in Palestinian peasant society. To have a large number of children was a sign of a man's health and wealth and of Allah's generosity. Infant mortality was high, and ill-health and exhaustion resulting from frequent pregnancies were the lot of most women.

Even though women's status improved once they had borne sons, they were never secure. Husbands were free to mistreat their wives, using as weapons the ever-ready threats of remarriage or divorce. Fear of the unhappiness, disgrace and economic distress these would bring could trap women in relationships of misery and powerlessness. Umm Fawwaz explained why, in her view, men were so ready to exploit their power:

> Men's attitude to women comes from their upbringing. When a man gets married, everyone says, 'Don't let your wife control you'. That is a man's most basic fear. His manhood is measured by how well he can control his wife.

She was scornful of the way women connive in their own oppression:

> Most women in our society are stupid. They are afraid of their husbands, and care more about them than they do about their children. 'Your father will beat me, he will divorce me, if I do such and such', they say. They don't have personalities of their own. Look at how my mother stood by and watched while my father destroyed my life by marrying me to my no-hoper of a husband. I hate her for it now. And me: for thirty-eight years I never did anything my husband would disapprove of. Whatever I wanted to do, I wrote and asked him first, even though he had more or less abandoned me. I only escaped from this when I went to America and saw with my own eyes how little he cared about me and the children.

Umm Fawwaz succeeded in managing her life in her own way, and is defiantly proud of the fact. Despite the constant opposition of her brothers and sisters, she sent her children to university and amassed considerable wealth through far-sighted property dealing. She admitted, 'In some ways it was easier for me to do what I thought was right, because I didn't have a husband at home to worry about'.

The threats of remarriage and divorce may have been effective weapons against women, but neither was actually practised very often in Palestine, at least in recent times. The Prophet Mohammed sanctioned polygyny to ensure that widows would be provided for, and this is still the reason for some second marriages, though a more common cause is the failure of the first wife to bear sons. Polygyny was never supposed to be merely an indulgence of men's sexuality: Palestinians, like other peasant societies, have fairly puritanical ideals in this respect.

Where second marriages did occur, co-wives lived in varying degrees of harmony with each other. Umm Suleiman described how when her husband first remarried, her 'heart was black against him' and she refused to have anything to do with the new wife. Gradually, however, she had to establish relations with the second wife; they lived in adjoining houses their husband had built on his land, and their children were married to each other. 'It's no good throwing stones into the well you have to drink out of', she explained.

Divorce does not seem to have been common within living memory, and is not now. Some observers have thought that because divorce is so easy, there can be no stigma attached to it. In Palestinian society this was not true, or at least a double standard operated. It was for men that divorce was easy, and for them there may have been little stigma. Women were certainly devalued by it, because of the high value placed on virginity. However, if she was still young, a divorced woman would often quickly be remarried, as a second wife or the wife of a widower or divorced man. Her family did not want the burden of supporting her, nor did she want to live with the shame and low status of being single.

A woman's status and power reached a peak when her sons married and she stepped into the position of mother-in-law. Some of the restraints previously imposed on her were relaxed, and indeed mothers-in-law proverbially compensated for their years of self-denial by becoming tyrannical and officious. Folklore recognised that conflict was inherent in the relationship between bride and mother-in-law, with sayings like 'A mother-in-law is a fever'. But the perpetual tension did not undermine the institution of patriarchal families, as mothers-in-law tended to be conservative: they had an interest in maintaining the system on which their privileged position depended.

3

The hold of the past: two personal stories

Tradition still shapes the lives and expectations of young people growing up today. Social structures grow out of particular economic conditions, but after those conditions have been transformed the superstructure of law, social power relations, role ideals and morality lives on for some time. Perhaps this is especially true of interpretations of women, which touch the very basis of any social system. In a patriarchal culture, control of women is fundamentally linked with men's (and women's) psychology. It forms part of individuals' construction of their identity, their self-respect, and their moral system, as well as giving them their acknowledged place in the social hierarchy. A transformation of outlook at this unconscious level is bound to be a slow process. So the subordination and seclusion of women, which were economically logical and practicable in a pre-industrial agricultural society, survive in the industrialised economy of occupied Palestine.

In rural areas and among the less educated, traditional role models still dominate, though with some modifications: young women are more likely to be educated than a few years ago, more likely to go out to work, and probably do not marry until eighteen or twenty. Even for the most educated urban women with the highest social and professional status and the highest aspirations of personal liberation, traditional norms censor their behaviour. None can afford to ignore *'kalaam in-nass'* – 'people's talk' – as private and professional life for women are still dependent on social acceptance. For single women this means absolute conformity to custom. A few examples will illustrate how wary they must be of stepping over the

35

accepted boundaries. The most highly-qualified dentist in the West Bank had to continue living with her mother, though she would have preferred to live alone, because if she moved out people would gossip about her private life, and she would lose her patients. The head of a university department found it difficult to find a landlord who was prepared to rent a flat to her as a single woman, and now her neighbours watch her every coming and going. A writer and political activist told me she was 'grateful' that due to an administrative mistake she had attended school in a small town rather than in the freer atmosphere of Jerusalem: the experience taught her how to pretend 'feminine' demureness, an essential skill if she wants to win support for her political and social ideas.

Such women make the deliberate choice to accept constraints on their personal lives for the sake of their professional or political activities. For many others there is no choice; traditional behaviour is forced on them, overpowering their search for lives of greater freedom. The second of the following speakers has tried to construct her life around her own moral convictions and emotional needs, but has found that, as in the past, community opinion sees women as objects in the politics of the patrilineal family. She is committed to the rights of individuals, but as a woman has little power to assert her belief. For the first speaker, the struggle between old and new ways is internal. Intellect and will point her towards existential freedom, but she finds she cannot escape from the deep-seated conservatism instilled by her upbringing.

Nuha's story: a divided upbringing

Thirty-five-year-old Nuha is a member of one of Jerusalem's prominent political families. Her upbringing could stand as an illustration of all the struggles Palestinian women of her generation are going through. Her progressive brother urged her towards social and intellectual independence and political responsibility, and helped make her the respected professional and development activist she is today. But her mother was pulling in the opposite direction, determined to shape her into an ideal daughter according to the strictest norms of conservative Jerusalem society; according to Nuha's account, this is what she really is beneath her beautiful and apparently confident exterior.

I had a lot of conflict with my mother, I have to confess. She was a very strong woman, who always thought she knew best. She had a strong sense of her position in the family hierarchy, and felt we should obey her because she was our mother. Perhaps if she had had any other outlets for her energy, she wouldn't have had to prove herself in the family so relentlessly. But in the years around 1948, when lots of women were finding roles for themselves in social work – in first aid units, or helping refugees and war orphans – mother had her hands full with her first three children. Later, when the people's most urgent need had passed, she didn't think of getting involved. The only theatre for her strong personality was at home. Perhaps she was compensating for her lack of education. By the 1950s women must have been suffering, I think, from their inferiority in education compared with their husbands and children and the world around them.

My mother had left school at the age of fourteen, when her father said to her, 'Now you are a young woman, you can't go outside without covering your face. Either you must wear a veil when you go to school, or you must stay at home'. My mother chose not to go to school, rather than wear a veil. I don't think she refused as a matter of principle, I think she just thought it was ugly.

Her own mother belonged to the last generation of women who never went out unveiled. I think an important factor in the decline of veiling must have been the involvement of bourgeois women in social work after 1948; a veil would hinder your freedom of movement and inhibit communication with people. None of my aunts was veiled when I was a child. Indeed, all the women I saw around me were dressed in the height of fashion. I remember them in long, full, white skirts, and short-sleeved linen blouses, with their hair permed. Although my mother was so religious, she was always beautifully dressed. I've got a photograph taken on her honeymoon in 1945 which shows her wearing a skirt that doesn't come past her knees. What a complete break away from her mother's generation. I wonder what men thought of it? Unfortunately I never asked my mother much about her life and the changes she saw. I didn't become interested in women's issues until after her death seven years ago. I was only interested in politics.

My mother derived her view of life from the very conservative environment in which she grew up. Her whole family lived together in one big house, each of her brothers taking one corner as he married. They were all dominated by her strict and authoritarian father. I expect her mother was illiterate. Until my mother married, this was her world. She learned from it a strong and literal sense of righteousness. Her one aim in life was to bring up her family in the right way and ensure that her children had unblemished reputations.

Reputation, honour, they are almost the same thing. Honour was for her an image that had to be perfected. It was a matter of behaviour, not of inner state. Everything had to be simplified to fit the image. Anything that didn't fit, she didn't want to know about. Neither mundane details of everyday life nor individuals' inner feelings were of interest to her. She taught me the rules of how to behave: the words *'haram'* (it's forbidden) and *"iib'* (shame) were thrust at me constantly. But she didn't think it necessary to explain the rules to me. As I grew up I was fenced in by taboos whose meaning and purpose I didn't understand.

I was quite unprepared for my first encounter with the invisible wall that separates the sexes. I was eleven years old. I used to play with the other boys and girls whose houses shared a common courtyard with ours. One day one of the neighbour boys gave me a flower. We were playing some game, I can't remember what, and it was just a wild flower he had picked up. One of my brothers reported the scene to our mother. At once I was snatched away from the group. The next day I found myself standing on our balcony, looking down on my former playmates, my ears echoing with the command that I must not play with boys ever again. I had no idea why this had happened to me. All I knew was that my greatest pleasure, playing with my friends, had been taken away.

My first menstrual period was equally mysterious. We had a house in Jericho. There I was allowed more freedom than I had in Jerusalem and I enjoyed riding a bicycle. When my mother saw the first signs of my period, she tried to tell me that the bleeding was caused somehow by my bicycle. Her instinct was to interpret it as my just punishment for doing something so unlady-like as to career around on a bicycle when I was nearly grown up. When the signs persisted, she had to admit to herself that I was menstruating, but she never explained to me what it was. She became very sad and serious, and told me what to do about it, but that was all. She made it into a dreadful, frightening experience for me.

To women of my mother's generation, menstruation was a sign of danger. From then on I had to be protected against the shameful and horrible possibilities of sex. My mother never discussed sex with me, but I've asked her sister how she feels about it, and I suppose my mother felt the same. Every time my aunt sleeps with her husband, she feels she has fulfilled an unpleasant duty. To her, sex is something terrible, evil and nasty. She would much rather not have it at all. This is what she and my mother learned from their upbringing, and they have never known anything different.

For someone with this horror of sex, the thought of any of her children having any remotely sexual experiences as teenagers must have been the end of the world. Even my brothers became the objects of my mother's anxious protectiveness as they reached puberty and became aware of sexual needs. She wanted to steer clear of the whole business. As for me, she had to guard me absolutely, every step I took, from the least breath or suspicion of sexual feeling.

My brother Faisal was encouraging me to be intellectual, independent and strong. His expectations of me were high, but I was willing to make all the effort in the world to live up to them. I adored him, because he treated me as an intelligent human being, not just as a little girl. I remember when I was eleven or twelve he used to read a lot, late into the night, and I used to sit up with him. He was reading Sartre, de Beauvoir, Kierkegaard, the Existentialists who were the fashion at that time. If he came to a passage he didn't understand, he would read it aloud and ponder it. I would struggle to understand with him; I wanted to be involved, to show him I was not a fool. I got very frustrated – twelve years old and trying to understand Sartre!

Our mother was jealous of my devotion to Faisal, and distrusted his influence on me. She was trying to make a model daughter out of me. I should have joined her in her busy social life among the ladies of Jerusalem. It was the custom for the women of her circle to hold regular 'at homes' for each other. You dressed up and put on your make-up and came to sit demurely round the edge of the salon drinking coffee or tea and eating pastries. For many of the women this was their only social life outside their families. Most of the talk was gossip and scandal. There was never, never any intellectual conversation.

I dreaded these gatherings as I would dread hell! My mother wanted me to go to them, so that I would be seen by all the ladies who would soon be looking for brides for their sons. Arranging marriages was half the point of the meetings, and that was why I hated them. I refused to go and be inspected from top to toe, watched to see if I knew how to walk nicely and behave prettily. The women were not interested in knowing anything about me except whether I fitted the image of a good wife. Although I had no other social life, I generally refused to accompany my mother. If I was very angry with her, I even refused to come into the salon when it was her turn to entertain. I earned the reputation of being a social failure who preferred her books to people: this was embarrassing for my mother and reflected badly on her.

I knew there were other kinds of life, out of my reach. Some girls of my age were enjoying themselves. They invited me to parties, but I wasn't allowed to go. And I saw Faisal and his friends leading the sort of intelligent life that was only permitted to boys; they were always visiting one another's homes to discuss serious interesting subjects or simply to talk and laugh together.

At least my mother was not against my education. She believed it was leading to a certain desirable conclusion: after I had graduated from a reputable school, a nice young man from a good background would appear to marry me. Unfortunately, nothing worked out according to her plan. It was 1969 when I finished school, only two years after the beginning of the occupation. No one was thinking about getting married. Many young men had left the country. With no suitor presenting himself, my mother agreed that I could go to Birzeit, which was a two-year college at that time. It was nearby, I wouldn't be out of her reach. I was seventeen, and in experience still a child. As I got on to the bus the first day, my mother gave me her final instructions: 'No sitting under trees with men! Especially not in a place where people can't see you. I don't want to be hearing any stories about you; and you know the best way to keep your name clean is to avoid mixing with people too much. Understand?'

In fact, in her aim of bringing me up to be modest and virtuous, she had succeeded as well as she could possibly have hoped. Her ideas of right and wrong were cemented deep inside me. On an intellectual level I rejected all her premises, but when it came to putting my own ideas into practice, I found I was paralysed. The voice that I had heard all through my childhood was now coming from inside me, crying 'No! No! *Haram!* Shame!' I couldn't imagine myself having a boyfriend, and even disapproved of those girls who did – mostly Christian girls and some Muslims from the city of Nablus, which was less conservative than Jerusalem. I saw young men looking at me, but I never allowed myself to respond. At the most, I might be attracted to someone for a day or two, but as soon as I began to imagine the consequences of getting involved, I froze. The idea of going out with him, being seen with him, and being talked about, was like a nightmare.

My two years at Birzeit ended, and there was still no sign of the expected queue of suitors. My reputation of being dedicated to education had persisted, and potential mothers-in-law didn't know how good a housewife I would be. It was a big disappointment to my mother, but as she believed in education as well as in marriage (and didn't see that in our society there's a contradiction between the two) she allowed me to go to finish my degree at the American University of Beirut.

How could she reconcile my going off alone to the decadent westernised city of Beirut with her concern for my honour? I think Beirut was so far from Jerusalem, it was like a different world. As long as nobody from Jerusalem saw what I got up to in Beirut, my 'honour' would be unharmed. It was honour-as-image again, an image that had to be sustained in my mother's social world but not elsewhere. She was highly thought of in Jerusalem. She was elegant, modern, graceful and assured at the diplomatic functions she attended with my father. She repaid society for its commendation of her by endorsing its ideas and standards. Whatever was current in her time and place, she accepted. It was the custom among her Jerusalem circle to send daughters away to be educated, so she could do it too. Once I got to Beirut and she found that it was usual there for men and women to mix freely and go out together at night, she accepted that for me as long as I was there. Once I got back to Jerusalem, it would be a different matter.

Nuha's much-loved brother Faisal was in Beirut, working as a political officer in the PLO. He opposed the romantic militarism prevalent among Palestinians at the time, believing instead that victory would be achieved through patient education, information and diplomacy. Under his influence Nuha developed her commitment to the national cause but also her critical distance from the conduct and tactics of the PLO. At the same time Faisal was encouraging her to overcome her shyness.

I started struggling to get over my fear of intimacy and take the risk of opening myself up to people. Among Faisal's closest companions was a fellow Palestinian, Jamal, who was one of the best-known student leaders at the time. He was interested in me, and I liked him, but I was terrified of getting involved and making a fool of myself. He was a man of the world, older than me, sophisticated, famous. 'Why did he single me out?' I wondered. 'Just to make my life a misery? Because he likes my brother?'

He persisted in his attentions, and gradually I began to feel something for him. I was the envy of all the girls in the university. One evening I was sitting in Faisal's house with a book open in front of me, but I couldn't focus on it. I was battling with the problem of Jamal. He had become a challenge. I had reached a point where I had to find out whether I could cope with a relationship. I sat there talking with myself: 'Shall I? Shan't I? If I approach him, I will make myself ridiculous. But I've got to break through this barrier sometime. No, I can't'. Then I realised, 'I've got to end this miserable situation one way or another. I've got to face him. It's a risk but I've got to take it.' I decided to go and find him, at once, and tell him what I was suffering. It took more courage than anything I have ever done.

I rehearsed the scene in my imagination as I hurried to the restaurant where he normally spent the evenings. I was steeling my nerves, mustering all my resolve as if I were on my way to the scaffold. I threw open the door, looked around the room – and he wasn't there. I went back to my hostel room, thinking 'Tomorrow is another day. Who knows, anything can happen.'

This all took place on a Friday evening. On Saturday, my brother was killed. As if someone was planning it, deliberately.

The death (in a car accident) of the brother who had meant so much to her was a tragic blow. Nuha withdrew into herself, near collapse for months. She lost touch with Jamal, whom she now remembers with warmth but some wryness.

Recently I heard news of Jamal that shocked me deeply. Apparently he allowed his mother to find a girl for him to marry. The poor thing, twenty-two years old, was sent over from Jerusalem to join him in Amman, and after one week he left her. I was very angry when I heard this. He had always claimed to be modern and revolutionary in his ideas about marriage, talking about freedom and equality in relationships. How could he treat a woman like this? Men are extraordinary. They revert back to tradition so easily when it suits them. I'd always been slightly distrustful of Jamal's fine words. He had a lot of casual relationships which didn't seem to me to match his ideals of respecting women. Now my suspicions are confirmed. If ever I meet him again, however nice he is there'll be an element of scorn in my feeling for him: I despise a man who can treat women so badly.

I've never been attracted to the idea of marriage. None of the married relationships I've seen has inspired me, and I've never seen what I could put into a marriage or get out of it. I don't understand how our parents in this society expect girls to accept marriage at all. All our lives they teach us that men are dangerous and sex is dirty. How do they expect us to fall into someone's arms the minute we leave school, saying 'Take me, I'm yours'? The more education a woman has, the less easy it is for her to accept marriage. While I was in Beirut I had several proposals, but none that I considered accepting. One was from an engineer who knew my uncle in Kuwait. He heard about me there, thought I sounded like a good match, and came all the way from Kuwait to Beirut to take a look at me. He telephoned me:

'Can I meet you?'

'Why? We don't know each other.'

'Er, I've got a message from your uncle.'

'My uncle never sends me messages.'

'Can't I meet you anyway?'

'You're wasting your time. I'm not looking for this kind of thing.'

'I've come all the way from Kuwait.'

'Nobody asked you to.'

He was not to be put off, so I arranged to meet him in a café and told him what I would be wearing. I wasn't sure whether to go, but I happened to meet Jamal in the road outside the cafe, and so I asked him, 'Come and have a coffee with me.'

'What's going on? You've never invited me before.'

'Never mind, just come in.'

There he was, the engineer. He'd imagined me sitting alone, waiting for him. When I came in accompanied by a man, he didn't realise I was the woman he was looking for. I was able to examine him. Just as I'd expected, he was quite unattractive. No reasonably attractive man would have to use these mechanisms to find a wife, would he? I didn't speak to him, and when I got home from classes that evening the phone was ringing.

'Where were you?'

'I was there, you didn't see me. Doesn't that prove something?'

He came to see me at home, and for two hours I really laid into him. I poured out on him all my anger about the way our society treats women. More than my own anger, the anger of my whole generation. He sat mopping his brow, speechless. As he left he said, 'That wasn't very nice of you'.

'Nice! It wasn't nice of you to come! What made you think I wanted you? What made you think I wanted to marry at all? How do you know I haven't already got a boyfriend? Why did you think I was sitting here just waiting for you to come along? That's not nice, it's totally insulting.'

My personal happiness has always been inseparable from my political beliefs and the political environment. In my twenties the hope that one day we would have a country kept me going and made up for my sense of helplessness in personal affairs. In the mid 1980s I've seen our existence Palestinians become more and more precarious, and I've sometimes felt weak, hopeless and futureless. Sometimes I've wished I were married; I've longed to have a partner to help me bear the burden of disappointment and suffering. But it's no good hoping for marriage now. I'm thirty-five and way past the age for it.

In any case, I am more often grateful for my independence than sorry for my loneliness. My brother gave me the ambition to be a free human being, free in the sense of assuming my own destiny, freeing myself from intellectual, social or political domination. This does not mean individualism. Freedom, he said, is a relationship, not a private possession. I often hear his words in my mind as I struggle to find the meaning and freedom of my existence. I must practise his kind of freedom, disentangle myself from the state of personal and political alienation I have got myself into and find ways of communicating with the people whose destiny I ultimately share. I am better now at opening myself up to people than I was ten years ago, but my mother's teaching still has a strong inhibiting influence. I have plenty of opportunity to meet people, through my work here and abroad, but if the idea of a sexual relationship comes up, I find I cannot venture into it. However much I try to reason with myself, I still react with the feeling my mother taught me, that sex is the deadliest sin. My bodily needs are still subjugated to my spiritual ones, as she conceived them. In my feelings about religion in general I can still see my mother's power. I have tried to rebel, but I keep coming back into the fold. From time to time I feel a need to pray, which reminds me that I still believe. In praying, I bend all the way down and touch my forehead to the floor as if I'm confessing to God my weakness. As I perform this act of humility, I feel that I am expressing my real self – without pride, rebelliousness, and pretences to modernity, I'm still the dutiful Muslim girl my mother made me.

Huda's story: putting children first

Huda believes that children have a right to grow up in an atmosphere of love and emotional security, and she feels that she herself has a right to the emotional satisfaction of having her children grow up with her. Such ideas would cause no stir in the West, where individuals' emotional needs have long been given priority. In the West, the mother's bond with her children is usually considered to be more important than the father's, and the best interest of the child is the one consideration in custody cases following divorce. But Huda, abandoned by her husband, has found no support for her determination to bring up her daughters herself. On the contrary, she is opposed by the weight of patriarchal institutions and tradition on all sides.

First, the law is against her. In the West Bank personal status is ruled by the Jordanian version of Islamic law. This assumes that children belong to their father's family, and though in the case of divorce it provides for them materially by requiring the father to maintain them, it does not concern itself with their emotional well-being. The mother is granted custody only at the discretion of the judge, and loses it if she remarries. Certain that she would lose her daughters, Huda refuses to contemplate bringing a divorce action against her husband, so she remains dependent on him. Her parents and brothers give her little support; they have no sympathy with her love for her daughters, and are more concerned with the wound their honour has sustained through the breakdown of the marriage. In addition, she faces the hostility of the village near Nablus where her husband has sent her to live. She is a city woman living alone and bringing up her daughters with city ideas. The village people perceive her as a threat to their moral standards and close ranks defensively against her.

Huda's family fled from Haifa in 1948, and she grew up in Amman, Jordan, where her father owned a restaurant.

My father is proud that although he never finished school himself, he has educated his sons and daughters and let them do what they like and marry whom they like – all except me. I was only fifteen when my aunt's friend Ziad came to my father and asked him, 'Have you got a daughter I can marry?', and my father said, 'Yes, you can have Huda'. He trusted Ziad, because he came from the same village as my aunt. All I knew of Ziad was his face, and that much I didn't like. He was fifteen years older than me, and married with a son. He was working as a car dealer in Germany. His wife refused to go and live with him there, so he had divorced her and was looking for another. When I came home from school one day and my father said, 'Ziad has asked for you and I have accepted him', I said, 'No!' I refused to accept him. I was clever at school, and all I wanted was to come and go with my friends like other girls of fifteen. I cried and refused to eat. 'I'm afraid', I said.

'Don't worry', my father answered. 'Ziad is a good man and he will be kind to you.'

'Huda is too young to marry', my mother cried, and my father shouted at her:

'Well, she's getting married. Ziad asked for her, and I'm going to give her to him.'

'He's already married', I said.

'Never mind!'

'He has a son.'

'Never mind!'

'I'm a city girl, but he's a peasant and can hardly read or write.'

'Never mind. He will get you educated, anyway, in Germany.'

My father really believed this. He never tells a lie himself, so he believes what people tell him. When he said, 'I'm doing this for Huda's sake. I know what is good for her better than she does herself', the whole family had to agree with him because he was the authority in the house. My protests were no use.

I lived in Germany for five years, and had four daughters one after the other. Then I brought them back to Amman, and we moved in to live with my parents, so that Ziad could save enough money to buy some land and build a house for us. At least, that's what he said he was going to do, but I soon found out that he had a different idea in his head.

My relatives in Damascus heard that every time Ziad made a trip down from Germany with some cars to sell, he was visiting a certain woman in Damascus. He was telling her, 'My wife doesn't understand me, she is bored of me, we don't want each other any more. I need a woman who understands me, to come and share my life in Germany'. When someone came to me in Amman and told me this, I didn't believe her.

'What wicked talk! Ziad is saving his money so that he can build us a house.'

'Well, he's telling this woman that he wants to marry her. I'm just trying to help you. Here's her address.' I said to my mother, 'Before we start making a fuss, we had better go and see whether this story is true or not'. So we set off for Damascus at once in a taxi, me and my mother and the four little girls. Ziad's brother came with us, so that the woman would believe our story. We went to the address I'd been given, and as we arrived the woman was at the door and saying to us, 'I am the fiancée of Ziad. Who are you and what do you want?'

'I am his wife, and these are his daughters.'

'Oh yes, the wife who doesn't want him. He told me all about you.'

I was only just over twenty, remember, and ignorant of the world. I was amazed to see her, and to realise that she loved him and was expecting to marry him, when all I'd been thinking of was buying some land and building ourselves a house. I could see that Ziad had told her just the same things as he had told my father, and she believed every word. I tried to warn her, but she wouldn't listen to me.

'Don't believe him!', I said to her. 'Look what has happened to me. He said he loved me, and took me to Germany, and then he stayed out all the time and hardly even came home to eat. You are young and beautiful and you could marry well. If you accept him, you will fail as I have failed.'

I felt ill with shock. When I got back to Amman my family said, 'Well, you must ask him for a divorce. He will take the children, and you can come back and live with us like a girl again. You are still young. You can go back to studying, and make new friends, and then marry whoever you like. We made a mistake giving you to Ziad, but it's not too late to undo it. Ziad has done wrong, he lied to us, and his daughters are his responsibility. We don't want to be bothered with them.'

How could they expect me to give away my babies? I didn't know what to do. I went and asked all kinds of people for advice, but they all said, 'Yes, you have to give up your girls. Ziad must take them and you must marry again.' My father, my mother, my brothers, all of them were angry with Ziad because they had trusted him and he had betrayed them. Arabs say the worst kind of traitor is the one who betrays 'your food and your salt'. Ziad had accepted the generosity of my family, then he made fools of them all. I admit that they had a right to punish him, but it was wrong to be thinking as they were of nothing but getting their revenge on him. They didn't pay any attention to my feelings or to the girls' welfare. 'He must divorce you, take his daughters and goodbye. We are prepared to look after you, but not them.'

I said, 'I am going to keep my babies. They need me. It's their mother who looks after children best. The Syrian woman wouldn't care for them as well as I can. It's not my fault or theirs. It wasn't me that chose Ziad, it was you, and you must take the consequences.' But all my family opposed me. My brother Mazen said, 'You've got a choice. Either you stay with us, by yourself, or you and your daughters must get out, now.'

They tried to convince me I was being foolish. 'You're too young, you don't know the world. You'll suffer for your daughters' sakes for a while, then they'll grow up and go to their father anyway, and you will have lost everything. Treat him as he treated you, an eye for an eye.'

I collected the children's clothes together and left. I had no money and no home. The only person who was prepared to help me at all was Ziad's brother.

Ziad was furious when he heard that I had left my family, and astonished too. How could they let me go out into the world by myself? His idea had been that my family would be happy to keep me and the girls, especially as we had been living with them for two years; then he would have been able to forget about us, and just send a little money each month to pay for our food. At least if they didn't want us, he had assumed that I would divorce him and send the girls to him for his Syrian woman to look after. The one thing he had not bargained for was that he would have to pay rent and enough money for us to live by ourselves in Amman.

Ziad did not want to initiate a divorce himself, because according to their marriage contract he was committed to paying a large sum of 'deferred *mahr*' in compensation, and his financial resources were already stretched to pay the marriage settlement for 'his Syrian woman'.

After a few years he built this house in his home village, Sarra, and told me I must come and live in it. He didn't want it to be said that a wife of his ever wanted for anything. In Amman he couldn't support me and I depended on help from my family (who had relented a little towards me). In Sarra, our life would be cheaper.

I didn't in the least want to move from the city where I grew up to this tiny village; I didn't want my daughters – five of them by now – to grow up to be peasants. But I had to accept Ziad's orders. The whole row with my family blew up again, worse than before. They refused to accept my moving to the village. In Jordan, people have the idea that life here in the West Bank under occupation is very dangerous. They are afraid of the Israeli settlers and soldiers. My family said, 'You're still a young woman. You can't go and live in the West Bank by yourself. You can't manage the responsibility of five girls, so far away from us. And the people there, they're peasants: how can you live with them? If you go and live over there, we will never come and visit you.' I answered, 'I will live wherever my children live', and so we came here.

That was eight years ago. Now that I've experienced life here, I sometimes think that perhaps my parents were right. It has been so difficult for us. It would have been better for me to stay with my family, and it might really have been better for the children if they had come here without me and been brought up by a village woman.

When we arrived, the village people didn't want us at all. They said, 'Who is this person Ziad married, and now he doesn't like her?' They all knew about the Syrian woman. 'This Huda is a city person, what is she doing in our village?' Ziad's first wife is still here; she walks past our house every day. She is very bad to me, so is his mother. They spread gossip about me, especially when I am away visiting Amman. Other people are quite good to me, but they don't really like me, because I am bringing up my girls by myself.

I've tried to understand the women here and make friends with them, and I would succeed better if it wasn't for the men. Men here spend very little time at home, but all the same they expect to have complete control over everyone and everything in the house. They say to their wives, 'We don't want that city woman Huda coming here, don't let her into the house.' The women are uneducated; some of them have never been out of the village. They let men rule over them and accept their orders: 'Don't do this, it's forbidden to do that, it's shameful to talk to this person.' The women don't know how to resist, they accept everything the men say.

Ziad's son Amin is just like the rest of them. He's only twenty but he loves to assert his authority over his sisters, my girls. He won't let them do anything. They can't even see their friends, except at school. A month ago we had a terrible row: the eldest, Najiye, went over to the house of some of her friends, and sat there for a while, just chatting. When he heard where she had been, Amin was furious. He said to me, 'I know you're a city person and you think differently, but I'm not having my sisters wandering around the village like that.' He fetched a group of his friends to talk to me – all this because my daughter wanted to visit her school-friend. 'If she wants to go visiting', he said, 'I must go with her. She's fifteen, it's not respectable for her to go alone. You with your city manners, you're a bad example to her. You should go back where you came from. We do things our own way here.'

The girls have suffered from being criticised like I am, because I am bringing them up the way I believe in, not like village girls. I teach them to eat at a table, not on the floor like people do here. They like dancing and singing, but these things are called ' *'iib'* here. I was brought up wearing short skirts; I'm not going to change, and I've brought them up to dress like city girls too. I don't mind putting a scarf over my head when I go out of the house, but nothing will make me wear a long dress like village women do.

When I visited Huda six months after these defiant words, she had given in to the pressure of village disapproval, which is increasing with the tide of Muslim revival. She was wearing a long dress, even in her own house, and apologised: 'I'm sorry, you see I've started dressing like a peasant'. Then she took me to her wardrobe and showed me what for her is the ultimate defeat – a long, plain blue dress, the *jilbaab* worn by adherents of the Islamic fundamentalist revival. Huda now puts this on whenever she goes for trips outside the village. She was alone in her battle for Western dress, for her daughters share the village's standards of propriety, and are relieved to see their mother dressing 'properly' at last.

How can I forget the life I lived in the past? I don't like village customs. Arabs bring their girls up to sit in their fathers' houses until they get married, and even after that they cling to their parents. I want my girls to be more like Europeans or Americans. If they learn how to travel and come and go by themselves and be independent, they won't have to call on their parents for help all the time. They will be able to cope with life. I want them to believe in themselves. I show them that I respect them; we discuss everything together at home.

We go to Amman for two months every summer, and we have such a good time there, when it's time to leave, the girls cry and ask why we can't live in Amman all the time. We have tried to go back to live there, in fact, but the Jordanian government has made a rule that West Bank people can only go to Amman for visits, not to live. It's supposed to stop people emigrating; the Jordanians are afraid that everyone would leave the West Bank if they had the chance. Although I was born and bred in Amman, I count as a West Bank resident now; Ziad has a West Bank identity card, and I am his wife, so I have one too.

When Ziad comes to visit us I quarrel with him, because he doesn't give us enough money, and anyway, there's no understanding between us any more. It's very hard for the girls. They don't know who to side with. I tell them, 'These are problems between me and your father, they are not your problems. You must love your father, he's the only one you've got and you may need him in the future. If I ever do leave you, you will have to get on with him. Besides, he will choose your husbands for you.' Although the girls know that Ziad doesn't care for me, they do love him. Now that they are nearly grown up, he enjoys their company, and I think he'd like to say to me, 'You brought them up, thank you very much, now I'll have them.' Sometimes, when the girls see how much I have suffered, and how he and I can't get along together, they say, 'Don't worry about us, go away and find someone new to marry.' But I say, 'No, for your sakes I can bear anything.' They don't really understand, they are too innocent and don't know what suffering life has in store for them.

They will be getting married soon. Then what will I do? This is what my family have always been afraid of. My mother says, 'You have no future. Tomorrow your daughters will leave school and they will marry peasants. You'll be left alone.' My brothers are the same: if ever I breathe a word of complaint about my difficult life, they retort, 'Well, you chose it.' They can't see why I stick myself here in the house being mother and father to the girls. 'You're just making Ziad's life easy for him. You're bearing his responsibilities, bringing up his daughters and sending them to school, keeping his house clean. Why are you doing all this for the man who treated you so badly, the man who threw you out when you were so young?' But what else could I do? I don't accept their point of view. Their only principle is that you must repay to people exactly what they have given to you.

4

Social change

Since 1948, but especially since 1967, powerful forces have been acting on Palestinian society in both directions, for and against change. Such forces would have arisen in any case, as the society adapted itself to inevitable membership of the industrialised world, but occupation by Israel has distorted them and created particular, often painful tensions.

Forces against change

Some features of the economic situation tend to hold women back in traditional or semi-traditional life-styles. One is the insecurity and low pay of men's wage labour, which perpetuates reliance on family land and the presence of women and other family members at home farming it. On the other hand, many women spend their days at home even when from choice or financial need they might prefer working, for Israel's economy has needed far larger numbers of male labourers from the occupied territories than female. Another practical barrier to women's leaving home is the low level of modern amenities in rural areas. With electricity in most villages available only for a few hours a day, water in many homes coming from a single courtyard well or tap, transport poor, and facilities for the care of children and the elderly few and far between, household work and care of the family are a heavy burden. Women interviewed in a survey of three villages carried out in 1981 put improved services as their most urgent requirement.[1] (As the researcher commented, the lack of amenities is not a straightforward result of occupation. Even under occupation, villages have some scope for development, but male village leaders do not have the same priorities as women.)

Families are large. The same survey found that among the married women in the villages, the average number of children was nearly nine. Fertility in fact rose during the 1970s, despite a drop in infant mortality and a rise in women's educational level, a factor that elsewhere is closely associated with a falling birth-rate. Palestinian families still perceived an economic logic in having more rather than fewer children. The insecurity of wage labour already mentioned is exacerbated by the absence of non-family welfare services: children are the resource who will support and care for old parents. As Israelis frequently and unhappily remark, the rate of population growth among Palestinians, though falling, is one of the highest in the world.[2]

From the 1950s onwards, thousands of Palestinian men left the occupied territories to find work abroad, returning to visit their homes only once every year or so. Some analysts have suggested that the status of the women left at home must have been improved by this phenomenon, as they found themselves obliged to take over roles formerly filled by men. Research has not in fact proved that this is the case. As acting head of her household, a woman does not automatically gain greater status or freedom. While some women no doubt enjoy their freedom from immediate supervision, many are consigned by the departing husband to the care of a male relative, or are even more restricted in their movements by their added vulnerability to gossip and criticism when they have no man to 'protect' them. When a woman is left as the sole provider, widowed or abandoned by a man who has stopped sending remittances from abroad, her household is likely to be among the poorest.

Cultural resistance to change

Cultural and psychological factors play a part in bolstering the traditional ideology and view of women. Conservative emotions, habits and convictions have been intensified by Palestinians' experience under Israel. Israel devotes much of its energy – military, political, economic, cultural and propagandist – to denying the existence of Palestine. Driven, therefore, to assert their national identity through every possible channel, Palestinians, like other nations in comparable situations, attach crucial importance to an idea of their national cultural heritage. Preservation of this heritage is an expression of political aspirations and a defence of national and individual self-respect; it also provides the comforting continuity of the familiar in an alien and threatening world. Not that the threat to traditional culture is due only to politics, or comes only from Israel. It is experienced by older cultures all over the world which are being engulfed by modern technology, media and consumption patterns. But for Palestinians the coincidence of the forces of modernisation with the force of Zionism seems to increase the painfulness of the confrontation between the old and the new.

For women, there are problematic elements in the 'national heritage' as usually conceived. To a significant extent the national heritage is seen as residing in 'the family' and the traditional roles of women. Many Palestinians see maintenance of the family in a fairly familar form as a positive contribution to the rebuilding of the nation, and this idea may be a brake on the liberalisation of attitudes. Strengthening of family ties is not just a matter of deliberate choice, but seems to be a response to political oppression. It has been observed that among the Palestinian population living inside Israel since 1948, the rate of cousin marriages has increased.

At an individual level, too, clinging to the familiar patterns of life at home is an instinctive response to personal threat. For men, especially the less educated and those who work as labourers in Israel, the family compensates for the alienation and humiliation of their experience outside. At work they are powerless, a despised social group, surrounded by a hostile foreign culture. At home they can maintain their self-respect, succoured by an environment whose values are their own. Honour and power over women and children might become crucial to men's sense of identity when they have so little else on which to base dignity and status. I have seen and heard of men using quite irrational pressure and violence against their daughters, in desperate efforts to force them to conform to traditions. If the daughter obeys, she is confirming her father's standing in his own eyes and in the eyes of his family and village. If she rejects his authority she is adding one more blow to his self-esteem.

Men are not likely to accept passively the attacks on honour constituted by the daily intrusion of Israeli soldiers into Palestinian streets and homes. Layla from Jabalya refugee camp in the Gaza Strip (see Chapter 9) commented on the results of this intrusion for women:

> In some ways, women are worse off now than they were before 1967. They were starting to dress more freely before the occupation, but when Israeli soldiers come into the camps, walk on the roofs, climb over walls, walk straight into our houses, we have no privacy. Men insist that we protect ourselves from being exposed to the soldiers' gaze all the time by putting on long dresses and covering our heads. Now most women in Jabalya wear long black skirts or *jilbaabs* and scarves over their heads. Before the occupation it was only in the very south of the Gaza Strip that women were so traditional. I never saw any of my relatives dressed like that when I was a child, but now they all are.

Images of women in art

Palestinians express their national identity (and membership of the Arab and Islamic world) artistically through poetry, music, dance, crafts, especially embroidery, and in the newly developing media of painting and theatre. (There is no Palestinian television station, and in the occupied territories no radio broadcasting facilities.) Artistic culture, like much else of today's popular activity, gathered momentum in the occupied territories in the mid 1970s, and it is an important unifying force in Palestinian life. One of its characteristics, however, is ambiguous for women. Palestinians' emotional and political responses to the loss of their land and security have produced a cluster of interlocking images of women, mostly of women as mothers – woman as mother of the nation, life-giver, nourisher, sufferer, defender of the home, source of love, identity and continuity. These symbolic images occur again and again in painting and literature. Feminists decry as retrogressive this elevation of woman-as-nature images; but many women, especially the older and less educated, find courage and strength in identifying themselves with the roles depicted. In saying 'My duty is to bear the sons who will fight', they find a meaning for their political and social oppression.

Forces for change

Strong the forces for conservatism may be, but the contrary

pressures for social change – industrialisation and education – are irresistible. Even the Islamic revival, while appealing to popular fears that 'westernisation' will bring social and moral disintegration, is in fact a movement to manage change rather than oppose it.

Economic change has eroded the old land-based subsistence farming economy, on which the *hamouleh* was based with all its hierarchical authority. Change began in the nineteenth century, when Ottoman reforms started to create a wage-earning class and brought money and market forces into the economy. By the 1940s as much as half the male workforce had left the land for jobs in the service of the British mandate or in the growing cities like Haifa and Jaffa. The movement was accelerated after 1948 when refugees who lost their economic base in land had to find new ways of surviving through education and wage work. Since 1967, emigration and the pull of jobs in Israel have further undermined inherited economic and power structures among Palestinians in the occupied territories who were not displaced in 1948. By the mid 1970s, even the remotest rural areas, which had been relatively untouched by the 1948 war, were affected.

Wages have largely replaced land as the basic source of wealth for Palestinian families. Free to sell their labour in the market, individuals are released from their economic dependence on the *hamouleh*. Young men and to some extent women can be independent and reject the *hamouleh*'s control over their progress through life. Umm Issa perceives the freedom of the post-occupation generation in her own village, Yatta, and her own family:

> Young people don't care about the *hamouleh* any more. They don't listen to the elders of the family. In the past everyone was dependent on everyone else. A young man had no choice. He had to obey his father because he had nowhere else to go, no chance of going away by himself and earning his own living. Now anyone who wants to can reject his father and go away and earn his own money and be independent, he doesn't have to accept his father's ideas. My two youngest sons are studying at university. Do you think they listen to their father?

Umm Issa says she deplores the new freedom, especially as it affects girls. None of the younger women I knew had any regrets, and many of the older ones, too, felt that loyalty to the *hamouleh*, at least in recent years, caused nothing but trouble: 'All *hayamel* did was pick fights with one another', an old midwife near Ramallah told me.

Education, as Umm Issa sees, is a great equaliser. All over the world there is close correlation between educational levels, of women and populations as a whole, and improved status for women. Respected by Palestinians for its own sake, and giving access to respected professions and jobs in the modern sector of the economy, education gives the younger generation a generally acknowledged superiority over the old, and gives women a chance of achieving status and power for themselves. Palestinians have experienced what can be described as an educational revolution in one generation, and the effects are bound to be far-reaching.

Changing expectations in marriage

The increase in individual wealth and the decline of *hamouleh* authority have brought new patterns and expectations of marriage. One result of the increase in size and flexibility of income is that Palestine is sharing in a world-wide trend away from extended multi-generational families towards nuclear families. The three-village survey cited above found that as many as three-quarters of the households were nuclear. A young couple can afford to set up home separately from the groom's parents, and prefer to do so. Without discounting the possible negative effects of this change for women, such as isolation and economic redundancy (which Palestinians do not yet widely perceive as problems) it seems clear that a smaller household improves a woman's position in several ways. It gives her a degree of autonomy in her own domain at an earlier stage of her life. It tends to create a closer and more equal relationship between husband and wife, which is visible in a narrowing of the age gap between spouses.

Palestinians experienced a dramatic rise in private consumption during the 1970s, though they are poor in public services. Improved material standard of living tends to reduce the desire for large numbers of children. Birth control is increasingly available, and from the upper classes downwards, young Palestinian women are choosing to have fewer children, with all the improvement in health and independence this brings. Young women now say that four or five children is a good size for a family.

Romantic love

As the personal relationship in marriage becomes increasingly important, young people are demanding the right to choose their own spouses. Relations between the sexes, love and the perfect marriage partner are frequent topics of conversation among young people, and the desirability of free choice is axiomatic – although for most of them the opportunities for meeting members of the opposite sex are still very limited, and the choice has to be made among partners selected by parents rather than from a circle of personal acquaintances.

Nonetheless, with greater freedom of choice, romantic love becomes a factor in marriage for the first time on a large scale. Arabic literature has been full of romantic love since before Islam, but the love celebrated in poetry had little to do with the practicalities of marriage and was not regarded as necessary for a happy life. Besides, love was a risk to a family's honour: a daughter in love either had already behaved shamefully, or was likely to. Now among professional people love matches are the norm. In rural communities romantic love is familiar from television, among other sources, but because of the separation of the sexes it does not occur frequently enough to seem relevant, and is still regarded, at least by older people, with suspicion. I asked Umm Jihad whether she regretted not having a great romantic passion in her life:

> No, it makes no difference in the end. Love like that is no guarantee that you'll be happy. I was terrified when I married my husband, because I hardly knew him and certainly didn't 'love' him, but he's a good man and we've been very happy together. And you see people who marry for love – Pft! after a few months of living together it's gone, and they're always arguing.

A more reliable sort of love is the kind that develops with time, if you have been sensibly married to a reliable person whose background you share. Among students, however, love is highly romanticised and no doubt romantically experienced, taking the place of the *hamouleh* as the modality of men's dominance over women. Marriage without love is scorned; but romance can be underpinned by considerable pragmatism. I asked twenty-two-year-old Aisha, whose ambition was to become a lawyer:

'Aisha, do you expect to marry for love?'
'Yes, all my five older sisters did.'
Me (*surprised*): 'Really? How did they meet their husbands?'
'Oh, they were all cousins of our family.'

Pragmatic or not, young people at the moment find that their expectations are clashing every day with the desires of their parents. As the old morality collapses, its economic rationale destroyed, a new one is emerging through innumerable inter-generational family disputes and rebellions. Parents still claim authority and the right to choose, or at least lay down criteria for, partners: a certain income or educational level, a certain status of family, and, especially, the same religion. Mixed Christian/Muslim marriages cause great distress and conflict. A girl is less likely than formerly to be forced into a marriage she does not want; on the other hand, it requires great determination and courage for a young person of either sex to marry against the wishes of his or her parents.

Egyptian soap operas, popular television viewing in the occupied territories, illustrate the new morality and the conflict it entails. The plots of several I saw revolved around the figure of a tyrannical father thwarting young lovers. The father is shown as a pitiful or comic figure, desperately trying to assert the authority he grew up to expect, unable to accept that it is now outmoded and impossible. The marriage he is trying to force on his child is derided as being selfish, greedy, snobbish, status-seeking – the very qualities, in fact, which would once have been accepted with pride by all the parties concerned, which were indeed the principal considerations in arranging a marriage. On television, of course, the father is defeated and love triumphs. In real life this does not always happen.

Migrants' marriage arrangements

The traditional method of seeking a wife through networks of family contact is still used by a significant sector of Palestinian society, namely men who have left the occupied territories to work abroad and want to strengthen their ties with home by marrying a girl from their own family or native village. In the summer or during the Ramadan holiday emigrants return and engage their families or business contacts in hastily looking for wives. The whole process of meeting, betrothal and marriage may be completed within a few weeks. If the man has been away a long time, he cannot be chosen as a son-in-law on the basis of personal knowledge of his character, as he would have been in the past, and money is now a significant factor. The attitude in the occupied territories to such marriages is ambiguous. They are desired, as jobs abroad are desired, because they represent wealth, freedom and opportunity. At the same time they are condemned. 'It's like selling girls to the highest bidder', I was told, 'and the girls themselves are thinking only of material advancement.'

Palestinian emigrants' wives face the same likelihood of isolation and restriction as women of other immigrant communities. A mythology has grown up around the phenomenon of marriages to Palestinians, particularly in the Americas, highlighting the dependence and misery of the wife thrown into a country and perhaps a language and culture that are strange to her, and the possibilities of exploitation and deceit on the part of the husband. It is often said in the West Bank that 'Palestinians in America are living the way we did twenty years ago'. Stories abound of how young 'imported' wives are kept more strictly under surveillance in their new homes than they were in the old. Huda told me how after all her husband Ziad's promises of installing her in a beautiful house in Germany and sending her to college, he in fact kept her closeted indoors. She was lucky in attracting the sympathy of a young German woman working in the bakery shop below the flat, who helped her to learn German and get a job in the bakery. In five years she hardly saw anything of Germany outside the walls of the building. Another village girl (Jamileh, see Chapter 5) said:

> My sisters live in cities in the United States. Their husbands are afraid for them so they are not allowed to go outside their houses at all except on Sundays when the men are home from work and they can take them out. Even if the doorbell rings, they don't answer it.

Sometimes women arrive in their new homes to find that their husbands have local wives or mistresses and want their Palestinian wives just to keep house and bear Palestinian children. Many of these American marriages are said to end in divorce, either because the wife is so dissatisfield that she comes home, or because the husband, having got used to Western women, is bored with his uneducated and submissive village wife. Whether or not unhappiness in migrant marriages is as universal as popular wisdom suggests, I certainly met many women who had personally suffered from this particular result of Palestine's economic situation.

Marriage arrangements of one village family

Traditional cultural forms are enduring longer in some communities than others, and sometimes being adapted to new functions rather than abandoned. The present transitional state, where apparently contradictory old and new patterns exist side by side, is illustrated by the marriage arrangements of one family in Beni Naim, a large village near Hebron, as I learned about them in 1985.

Beni Naim prospered in the 1960s and 1970s, as many of its men left to work abroad. (The village bus company was named 'El Dorado', in homage to the proprietor's small fortune made in Brazil.) Many of those who stayed at home earned a good living as craftsmen and small traders all over the occupied territories and inside Israel. With the money that flowed back, most families built themselves new houses, but the village was remote and lacking in communal services such as water, electricity and medicine. (The relative underdevelopment of villages compared with towns in the occupied territories is striking, especially given the small distances that separate them and the amount of individual wealth that was available for a few years. It reflects the planning vacuum and the obstruction of development imposed by occupation, and the inherited urban and individualist bias of pre-nationalist Palestinian politics.) In Beni Naim, the daily routine of women's lives had changed little, and the village had preserved its traditional social attitudes. But it had also shared in the nation-wide education revolution: whereas women of twenty-five were semi-literate, their younger sisters were in high school, and dozens of young men were graduating from the West Bank's universities and colleges. This will surely have dramatic and visible effects on the village's social organisation in the near future, but for the time being the old forms persisted. Despite the men's contacts with other villages and towns, in Beni Naim the traditional preference was still strong for 'putting on your face the mud from your own land' – that is, marrying someone from within the village community, even from your own family.

Forty years ago, a brother and sister married another brother and sister pair from a different branch of their *hamouleh*. Umm Suleiman bore several sons, but her brother's wife bore only daughters, and her brother eventually exchanged the oldest of these for a second wife for himself. In a spirit of competition, according to Umm Suleiman's sons, Abu Suleiman decided that he must marry again too. He chose the widow of his brother, who herself had four daughters. He justified the marriage as his Islamic duty: a man is required to support the widow of his brother, and marrying her is one common way of doing this. But the prior duty is to maintain your first wife and her children, and this Abu Suleiman could not afford to do. He effectively abandoned Umm Suleiman and her eight children, the oldest of whom left school at twelve to start working. The *hamouleh* mobilised all its power of disapproval and ostracism against Abu Suleiman, but 'he was obstinate'.

Although he had abandoned them, he was still his children's father and had authority over them. He sent his oldest daughter to marry a cousin living in a refugee camp in Amman, in defiance of her wishes and her mother's judgement. Events proved them right, as she found herself living in poverty in one room in the camp with eight 'horrible, uncontrollable' children, and was ill-treated by her husband. Her sister Munira was happier, being married into a family of neighbours in the village and living next door to her mother. Next Abu Suleiman was able to arrange the most desirable of all marriages, between his son Suleiman and the daughter of his brother – now also his step-daughter. Six years before I met them, Suleiman had married his cousin Halima, who within five years presented him with two daughters and two sons. Suleiman's third brother, who like Suleiman left school early and worked with him in his plastering business, tried to break away. He fell in love with a girl in Jordan, where he worked for a few years. But the relationship came to nothing, and he decided to satisfy the desires of the whole *hamouleh* by marrying one of Halima's sisters.

The remaining two sisters and two brothers illustrated the familiar fact that 'development' reaches men before it reaches women. The two sisters had only a few years' schooling and had hardly ever left home. They worked at home at knitting and embroidery (see Faatmeh, Chapter 8). The two cousins they would by tradition have been destined to marry were university-educated, despised the unfortunate girls, and had no respect for their father's wishes. They would have liked to find wives among their university contemporaries. Perhaps the educational inequality between the sexes will even out in a few years. The younger generation of girls, Abu Suleiman's second family and their friends, were nearly all attending school successfully and planning to follow in their brothers' footsteps to further education and careers.

The family illustrated the changing patterns in another important respect, the payment of *mahr*. In some communities, especially refugee camps near towns where work was fairly readily available for both sexes, *mahr* had almost been abandoned. Refugee families did not have the capital needed for large *mahr* payments. In addition, women were able to work and support themselves and so did not need the protection of marriage gifts. *Mahr* was seen not only as unnecessary, but also as humiliating to the woman, implying as it did that she was being bought. In Deheisheh refugee camp, only a few kilometres from Beni Naim, young women were proud to tell me that they and their parents no longer asked for *mahr*. The new habit had not spread into Beni Naim, where the rate of *mahr* payment was as high as anywhere in the West Bank or Gaza Strip.

In 1985, the normal cost of marrying a relative was between 2,000 and 3,500 dinars (£4,000–£7,000) and for a non-relative was 4,500–6,500 dinars. To raise this sum, which was over twice the annual income of most men, the groom's family had to resort to years of saving, the pooling of all the family's earning power, and borrowing from other branches of the family. Marriage was always expensive. In a village near Bethlehem in the 1930s it was reckoned to cost three years' of an agricultural worker's savings. In Beni Naim in the mid 1980s the rate was higher and people constantly complained about the expense, but they did not seem to see it as something that lay within their control. Munira said, 'It doesn't matter what people do in other places, we have to do whatever other people in the village do, and that's all there is to it.'

The decision of how much *mahr* should be paid was a delicate matter, as it had always been, involving the honour of all parties. When Halima married Suleiman, Abu Suleiman did not waive the *mahr* altogether, although he could have done this, standing as he did *in loco parentis* to the bride as well as being the father of the groom. To do so would have appeared to the village to be a slight on

Halima and exploitation of her fatherless state. So, 'to close the window against criticism', she received gifts at the going rate. When Munira married her neighbour, her father did waive the *mahr*: such magnanimity to a poorer family was seen as honourable.

Halima moved into her mother-in-law's house with some mattresses and quilts and some gold jewellery. The coins that her mother wore in her headdress were already outmoded, and Halima bought earrings and bracelets, like most brides of her generation. In the six years following her marriage, the village was prospering and the style of living changed. In addition to increasing quantities of gold, young brides expected their husbands to provide European-style furniture, whether they were moving into a room in his father's house or into a house of their own. Halima's cousin Suad, marrying a few years after she did, was given a bedroom suite. To an outsider's eye it looked bizarre – elaborate gilded furniture standing on a bare cement floor in a curtained-off corner of a half-built house. But it was the current fashion, and Suad was proud of it.

Two years later another cousin was engaged. She insisted on an inordinately high price. If she had been unwilling, this would have been understandable, but as she knew the groom well and loved him, nobody could understand why her demands were so high. She continually raised them – a power the bride's family had, because it would have been insulting and risked an honour feud if the groom's family had refused to pay what was asked once the betrothal had been agreed. The total of 5,000 dinars (£10,000) was made up as follows: 2,000 dinars' worth of gold jewellery; a *'kiswe'*, that is, clothes for the bride and her relatives, which included twenty-three dress lengths for her aunts and sisters and six evening dresses for her to display during the wedding; 500 dinars in cash, which she spent on more gold, cooking equipment and bedding; 800 dinars for a bedroom suite; and around 450 dinars for a wedding feast for several hundred guests.

This story indicates that Beni Naim people did not share the 'modern' interpretation of bride-price as a humiliation for the woman; on the contrary, this bride saw a high price as a positive indication of her status and value. Her dependence on men – on her father to consent to the marriage and fix the price, on her husband to provide her home and livelihood – was not questioned. In Beni Naim no alternative model existed, as opportunities for women to earn their own living within reach of the village were few, and no village women had yet left to live independently in towns.

The custom of *mahr* was kept alive in Beni Naim partly by a concern with status. In the past status was related to ownership of land, family origin and honour, and was thus fairly stable. In the free-for-all of the capitalist money economy it is shifting and closely bound up with money. Status seems to be a preoccupation of Beni Naim people (see the interview with Munira, Chapter 7).

Mahr has also had another more practical function in recent years. As material expectations have risen, the cost of establishing a home and family has increased rapidly, but none of the facilities through which couples in the West spread the cost and secure their future are available in the occupied territories. There are no commercial loans, because there are no banks except Israeli ones, which village people do not use much. The few building societies are those set up by professional associations for their own members, and they are not accessible to most village people. Hire purchase schemes are unknown and insurance is rare. It would be hard for a couple to accumulate by themselves the sum needed to set up home. The *mahr* has been an effective way of pooling available resources from the family and channelling them to meet this need.

Despite this usefulness, *mahr* is increasingly being seen as a burdensome custom and incompatible with belief in the equality of women. This emerged clearly during the *intifada*. As the uprising gained momentum, teenagers and women emerged as important actors. To participate fully they had to override traditional authority structures and customs which restricted their mobility and autonomy. This 'social uprising' was hailed and actively pressed forward, at least by the young generation who were taking the political lead. One of the traditions dropped was *mahr*. Severe financial hardship was hitting everyone in the occupied territories, and the setting aside of demands for *mahr* was proclaimed as a political act, a gesture of support for the young people who were fighting the occupation. Parental control of marriages was also reduced. After a year of the uprising, along with political achievements and terrible sufferings, young people were proud to list the number of recent marriages among their friends – love matches where previously insuperable social or religious differences had been accepted without opposition by the parents. The explanation of the new climate was that in the midst of violence and danger, traditions seemed less precious to parents than their children's lives and happiness. Whether the changes will be permanent remains to be seen.

5

Articulating the new freedom

With changes in the economy, education and the family opening up to them the world outside the home, and the political drama drawing them in as responsible actors, Palestinian women are well on the road to 'liberation' compared with their mothers, or women in many other Arab countries. The progress already made in this direction implies changes in the perception of women and in gender power relations, the sum of which is that women are accepted as being capable of functioning in the world outside the home. Implicitly, it is being conceded that they have the power to control their own sexuality; the assumptions that they are vulnerable to every man and that they will spread havoc wherever they go are dying. The absolute right of men to control them has been overthrown. With these perceptions of their own abilities and rights, women have collectively gained self-confidence.

Many women are benefitting from the new possibilities, but possibilities alone are not enough. Woman have to perceive them, organise around them, push them further, take them to less fortunate sisters. They have to reflect on the experience of the past, choose directions and formulate new demands. How are women articulating their opportunities of freedom? How do they see the future they are working for?

The Islamic revival movement

One conceptual framework in which some women are interpreting their new needs is Islamic fundamentalism. The revivalist Islamic movement often presents itself as a return to tradition, and is so perceived by some of its supporters, as well as outside observers. In fact it is a more positive movement, not merely longing to recreate an idealised past but trying to shape the future.

The Islamic revival began to gain ground among Palestinians, especially in the Gaza Strip, after the 1979 Iranian revolution, and it quickly became a considerable force in social and political life. The movement has several different threads, which are hard for an outsider to distinguish. At the popular level it mobilises fears of immorality, the collapse of the family, and social chaos, laying stress on the Islamic model of a cohesive, ordered, responsible society. Piety and traditional morality as responses to the 'corruption' of westernisation gain ready support, and long dresses and head covering for women are increasingly demanded in towns and villages where a few years ago Western dress – short skirts and bare heads and arms – was gaining acceptance. It was the rising tide of moralism in Huda's village, for example, that compelled her (see Chapter 3) to adopt long clothes. In response to the same pressure, one or two higher education institutions established on a more Western model in the 1970s or early 1980s have introduced separate classes for men and women.

At the centre of the movement are highly organised and disciplined cadres whose aims are political. For them, the revival is a revolution against the political, economic and cultural domination of the West. Its goal is the establishment of an Islamic state. This is conceived of as a modern state, able to play a role in the modern world but rooted in Arab history, and constructed not on the secular basis of a Western state but on a God-given model. It would have all the advantages of a modern state – economic strength, a high standard of living, political independence – with none of the perceived disadvantages of Western life. In capitalist states, cut-throat competition and individualism are seen as producing social injustice and disorder, and spiritual and moral emptiness, while socialist states are godless and morally hollow.

The sources of the Islamic movement's appeal are many. All over the world, people oppressed by colonialism, seeing their culture swamped by Western consumer values and their economies and politics controlled by corruption, absolutism and imperialism, look for ways to shape their fate in a world of their own making. For many of them the Islamic nationalism of the revival seems to be the answer. The Islamic movement draws its supporters predominantly from the urban lower middle classes – an emerging class who do not fit into traditional society and whose new aspirations for economic success and political power are frustrated. In the occupied territories, where the small distances and density of population blur the rural/urban distinction, support comes from educated young people in towns, camps and villages. The appeal of the revival was perhaps increased, before the *intifada*, by disillusionment at the perceived failure of the secular policies of the PLO to find a solution to the problem of Zionism. An indication of the size of the movement is that at Birzeit University, the most secular and politically active of the Palestinian universities, the Islamic movement had the support of one-third of the student body during the early 1980s.

The appeal of revivalist Islam to women

For outsiders it is hard to see what the appeal of the Islamic revival can be for women. What satisfaction is there in being obliged to dress in an almost uniform, joyless and constricting costume? The answer lies in the contrast between a concept of 'pure' Islam and the interpretations of Islam that developed through the centuries. This contrast has divided campaigners for women into two distinct camps, ever since the nineteenth century when a movement for the improvement of women's status in the Islamic world began in Egypt. On one side have been those who have seen Islam as inherently hostile to women and an obstacle to be overcome; on the other side have been those who taught that by returning to the origin and true principles of Islam, women would find their due status and proper role.

One of the features of the modern Islamic revival that attracts young women is the emphasis on those aspects of Mohammed's teaching that recognise women's rights and value, and the specific rejection of many of the accretions of peasant and tribal custom. For women from village backgrounds, revivalist Islam offers a far better life than *hamouleh* tyranny. For any woman rendered economically superfluous by industrialisation and kept idle by gender ideology, the new Islam offers a sense of purpose and identity. (In a similar way, evangelicalism and religious sisterhoods appealed to middle-class British women in the nineteenth century.) The movement encourages education and work for women, and their active participation in social and political affairs (albeit in separate, defined spheres). It assumes that a woman, protected by her Islamic dress and armed with self-control, can be responsible enough for her own sexuality not to need a man's protection at all times. The purpose of Islamic dress is to erect a barrier between a woman's sexuality and the outside world. Some urban women find that it is a positive weapon in their struggle for equality – a clear and universally recognised statement of a woman's refusal to be treated as a sex object. Islamic dress helps her to be accepted on equal terms with men in work and intellectual affairs.

Jamileh speaks for the many young village women who are finding in Islam support for their need to break out of oppressive village traditions. Seventeen years old, she lives in a small village north of Ramallah, close but relatively unaffected by town habits. The head of the family is her brother, who exercises his responsibility from the United States, keeping control by letters and phone calls, information from the network of other emigrants, and annual visits home. As Jamileh explains, though he may be adopting some American customs for himself, he is determined that his sisters must continue old traditions. Emigration probably strengthens this determination: his sense of his own dignity is still bound up with the family honour, which is located firmly in the village. There his young sister, living without the protection of a man, is especially vulnerable to dishonour and must be all the more closely guarded. Educated at high school and secretarial college, Jamileh resents his tutelage. She does not wish to enjoy 'Western' sexual freedoms or abandon her own culture, but she does see that greater freedom, financial independence and participation in national life are available to women like her as never before – and available within the protective and indigenous framework of revivalist Islam:

> There are many contradictions between true religion and village customs. Our Islam gives women many freedoms and rights, but most men don't read the *Koran* and don't accept that we have these rights. For instance, the *Koran* says that girls should be educated and then do something useful for society, but my brother refuses to let me go to university or to work. He thinks that girls in university are bad because they mix with men and do things they shouldn't. He doesn't understand what our Islam teaches us – that we must make the best of what opportunities we have. In an Islamic state, there would be separate

education for men and women; but as we do not have that, I can go to a mixed university as long as I am always protected by wearing a *jilbaab*. My brother is doing what village men have always done to women – trying to keep them in a cage, imprisoned by ignorance, so that they can dominate them. I don't really blame him: it is not him that doesn't want me to go, it's society that doesn't allow it. A man has to be very brave to allow his girls to go out and mix with men. There are only three girls in the whole village who have gone to university. One is my sister, who is married; she and her husband study together at the University of Texas. The other two are my cousins, who are studying dentistry in Syria. The whole village talks about them, and swears that nobody will want to marry them when they come home. What can a woman like me do? As men become more educated and know more about Islam, they will change. We just have to wait.

According to Islam, a girl can sit with a man if she is covered up except for her face and hands. But village custom says that a girl shouldn't be in the same house with a man, unless she has a husband or brother or father to escort her. I don't have any men in my family. This means that I can't visit any home where there are men living. I have one friend who has no brother and my mother lets me visit her, but she is the only one. Our society always thinks the worst. If people saw me coming out of a house where a man was, they would assume he was the reason for my being there. I can't have married friends come to visit me either, because people would think we were talking about shameful things that I'm not supposed to know about, not being married. These customs will change as the village becomes more educated.

Because she had completed secondary school, Jamileh was selected by the village to attend a course in 'life-cyle education' run by an American development agency to train girls to give some basic biological and health education to women in their villages. (She was chosen, in fact, by the elected committee of the sports club, the only representative body the village has.) The Imam of the village mosque is a Muslim Brother, an active adherent of the revivalist movement, and, like Jamileh, has a liberal view of what women are entitled to under Islam. He helped Jamileh to overcome village prejudice against the subject of her course, as she explains:

I wanted to be able to do something to help my village, and I know that there are many problems caused by women's ignorance of their bodies and of the basic rules of health. When the course was finished and I was ready to start a class in the village, I went to the Imam and explained the idea to him. He agreed that it was something important, and gave a sermon telling the people about it. Twenty-five women came to enrol. Straight away, there were problems. The first class had to be about the reproductive organs, and how babies are made. Village women don't know anything about their bodies. Even if they have been to school, there is very little sex education there. I'm sure if you asked my class at the secretarial college, most of them wouldn't know what menstruation is. Men don't want women to know themselves – if women are ignorant, men have more power over them. Women accept men's claim that talking about your body is shameful, because they think it is forbidden by religion. They can't read the *Koran* for themselves, they have to accept what men tell them. They know that the *Koran* tells you to cover your body, and they think this means it should be secret from yourself too. Actually there are chapters in the *Koran* all about our bodies and how they work, and we are told that we should understand how God made us. There is no contradiction, after all, between knowing about your body and covering it up modestly.

So, when I showed a slide picture of the woman's organs, the women in my class were astonished. They had never seen anything like this before, and thought it was wicked. They giggled and hid their faces in their scarves, then when the class was over they went running home and told their husbands I was teaching them rude and forbidden things. The husbands went and complained to the Imam. He sent for me, and asked if I couldn't please teach a little less detail? I explained to him that these things I was teaching were essential for women to know, and he agreed that God does not forbid such knowledge, and that the classes wouldn't make sense if I left anything out. So he spoke to the men again, not over the loudspeaker this time but privately inside the mosque. They accepted his word and my class came back again the following week quite happily.

For Jamileh, one of the important messages of Islam is that men should not have tyrannical power over women. There exists naturally a kind of equality which men should recognise and allow women to enjoy. At the same time she accepts with equanimity the idea that women's destiny is to marry and bring up children, and that to this end Allah created women with a very different nature from men. Very few Palestinians, whether Muslim or not, would question the supremacy of the family as the 'natural' social structure. But Jamileh is unusually explicit in her construction of social roles on gender differences:

There should be equality between men and women, but not sameness. In some areas of life, men need eighty per cent and women twenty per cent; in other areas women need eighty per cent and men twenty; put them all together, and you get one whole. Women have duties towards men, and to their families, but men have duties towards women too . . . Perhaps equality isn't quite the right word: Allah did put men above women. Women have some rights, but in many things it is men who make the final decisions. This is because they are stronger – not in their bodies, which isn't important, but in their minds. Women are nervous and rely too much on their emotions. In the matter of divorce, for instance, Allah knows that a woman might say, 'I divorce you', in a moment of anger when she didn't really mean it, so he didn't give her the power to divorce. He gave it instead to men, because men won't use it except in a rational way. It's true that if you look around you, you don't see men behaving in a perfectly rational way all the time, but that is because they have not freed themselves from ignorance and are not following the *Koran*.

Jamileh was the only Muslim Sister I talked to who was prepared to concede that 'equal but different' is a problematic concept when the characteristics allotted to men are the valuable attributes of mind, strength, leadership and independence leaving women at home with their children.

But is there a contradiction between freedom and the fact that you have duties to your husband once you are married? I don't think so. The important thing is having the right to choose in the first place. It is reasonable to give up some of your freedom when you marry, and commit yourself to obeying your husband if, and only if, your husband is your own free choice. You could say that whereas your duties are given to you by God, so you can't refuse them, your husband is given to you by your family, so you are not obliged to accept him.

Here we see the limits of the liberation offered by the new Islam. Though Islam opposes the village custom of total seclusion, by giving women some responsibility for themselves, the freedom allowed is pragmatic, not absolute. It is just enough to allow women to perform a useful function in the modern world. One of the principal charges made by opponents of the Islamic revival is that Islamic dress places women as sex objects just as surely as seclusion ever could. The Islamic concept of natural differences between men and women is still firmly patriarchal, and by Jamileh's account contains unchanged the traditional attitude to sexuality: 'Men can't help it, so women must be held responsible'.

I do believe that men and women should mix together as little as possible. They can't be simple friends with one another. We have a saying: 'When a man and a woman are together, Satan makes a third'. It is a natural characteristic of men that if they sit with a woman they always think about sex. You could be discussing an academic subject or a problem in the village, but the man's mind will be on sex. It doesn't always come out into the open but it is there, distracting him. The best way to avoid trouble is not to be together. Women are different, they can control their sexual feelings. If I was with a man, and showed him I wanted sex, it would happen. But if I don't want it, I can prevent it. That's why our society always blames the woman for any sexual trouble. It's not that she is to blame, but she is the one who is responsible.

Secular models of liberation

The majority of Palestinian women are seeking the referents for their new role within a secular framework, but their immediate demands are similar to Jamileh's: education, freedom and responsibility, mobility, the right to work, higher status within the family. These demands, which would have arisen anyway as a result of the economic and educational changes, are intensified by Palestine's history. Women are men's equals in their need to respond to their people's oppression. To contribute actively to the national cause, women have to shake off the social chains that have constrained them. They must have, if not equality, at least the freedom to leave their homes to work and share in public activities, the right to speak out when the occasion arises, and the right to overcome fear. They could have chosen to support the cause within their traditional sphere – protecting their children, supporting men, and nursing fighters – and many have done so. But for many more, the urgency of the need to resist Zionism and the new image presented by changing society have combined into a powerful impetus for change.

For many individuals and women's organisations, national liberation is the explicit goal of their demands for personal liberation. During the first decade of its existence, the PLO's armed struggle produced heroines as well as heroes, and these young women are an inspiration to women in the occupied territories, their pictures hanging on the walls of many homes. Nationalist action in the occupied territories takes the form of national social, economic and cultural development, but these require freedom of action almost as much as do military operations.

It has become a truism, a slogan heard from all political quarters, that 'women are half the nation; unless that half is active, how can we hope to win?' When causes are sought to explain why women are moving so rapidly forward into national life, the answer is often simply: 'the occupation' – an answer which in part refers to the economic changes imposed by Israel, but links them firmly with resistance. When I asked a young woman worker 'What has been the effect of the occupation on women's position?', it was her brother who replied with familiar rhetoric:

> The occupation is a two-edged sword. One edge injures us, the other edge injures the occupation by strengthening us. Unintentionally, the occupation has played an important role in liberating women. The Israelis' pursuit of their own economic interests has brought our women into the workforce. We have seen it as our national duty to help women join in the national struggle in this way. The conditions of our struggle demand women's participation, and this is why every liberated Palestinian man encourages women to liberate themselves.

This last sentiment is probably significant in relation to the way women are framing their demands: national political action is a goal acceptable to Palestinian society, including men, whereas the equality of women for its own sake would be harder to accept.

As well as being the goal of women's liberation, nationalist activity is often, as it has been throughout the twentieth century, the means through which individual women first become conscious of the need for freedom and begin to challenge their restrictions. Trying to participate in some common undertaking, women find themselves obstructed by social barriers. Examples are endless: one wishes to speak at a students' meeting, and finds she is crippled by shyness; another wishes to attend a meeting in the town but is forbidden by her father to be outside the house after dark; a third wants to join a local society but her husband complains that she is neglecting the house. Many women remain frustrated, but many more succeed in persuading men to loosen their restraint. The argument of national duty has probably helped many hesitant fathers to justify their relaxation of vigilance; this has certainly been true during the *intifada*. Zuleika Shehabeh, a founder of one of the first women's associations to pursue political goals in the early 1920s, remembers that 'nobody really objected when we threw off our veils. How could we work wearing them?'

Nationalist activity contributes to personal liberation in another way, helping to break down the isolation and ignorance that in the past has ensured women's acquiescence in patriarchal oppression. Coming together to discuss other things, women learn of one another's experiences, analyse and criticise their society, and formulate ideas of how things could be different.

Feminist education in prison

The extreme is the 'feminist education' women experience in prison, where they are thrown together with women from other parts of the community, witness one another's strengths and powers, and, most important, live without the inhibitions and burdens of men's presence. As one young ex-prisoner put it to me, unaware of the seriousness of her joke: 'The good thing about prison is that you don't have to keep jumping up and down to make coffee for men'. Salwa describes how the seven years she spent in prison from the age of sixteen opened her eyes both to the extremes and to the universality of oppression in Palestinian society:

> In prison, each one of us told the others the story of her life. I learned many things about the tyranny of men over women that my sheltered upbringing among the Christian community in Ramallah had never taught me. I'll tell you just one of the stories.
>
> One of the few non-political prisoners among us was a young woman who was ostensibly convicted for murdering her baby. She had been at work picking fruit one day when the owner of the orchard, an old man with married children, came and raped her. She was too ashamed and frightened of what her family would do to her to tell anyone. Then she discovered she was pregnant . . . She had the baby secretly, alone, and left it lying on the ground, hoping it would die. What else could she do? She was terrified she would be found out, so she turned for help to the only one of her brothers she was not afraid of. He called the police, but not in time to stop her other relatives coming to the house wanting to kill her, to avenge the family's honour. Her brother faced them alone, with a knife, and stopped them getting in. When the case came to court, the judge decided the man should pay financial compensation, but her family refused to accept it, as it would compromise their right to seek their own kind of justice – from her as well as from him. She was sent to prison for a year, more to protect her from her relatives than because the judge felt she deserved punishment. But what was going to happen to her next? I'm sure her relatives were just waiting for the day she was released to kill her.
>
> I heard stories like these, and at the same time I saw that women can endure the torture and hunger and suffering of prisons as well as men can. You can see why I became a fanatic for the cause of women.

Demystifying sex

Among progressives there is a clear demand that women, especially unmarried girls, should be allowed to know about sex. The ignorance in which they are still often kept is dangerous in the situations of free social contact in which they nowadays find themselves. Fadwa, a student of Birzeit University, explained to me why a group of students had formed a committee to hold meetings and lectures for female students on physical, emotional and social aspects of relations between the sexes:

> Our aim was to help girls to know how to behave in their relationships with men. Girls who come from villages have no idea how to behave appropriately, because they have never been allowed any contact with men before. We want to help them out of two dangers – the danger that their ignorance and desire to please will be taken advantage of, and the opposite danger that their lives will be made miserable by fear. Women are taught to be afraid of everything to do with men, they go around terrified but not really knowing what it is they are afraid of. They know they must not lose their virginity, but a lot of them don't even know what virginity is. They think they lose it by walking with a boy, certainly by letting him kiss her. Even when a girl is about to come to the university, the only advice she gets is, 'Don't talk with men'. So then the poor girl arrives, talks to a man, and immediately feels that she is a wicked harlot.

It is difficult to break down the fear and ignorance. With the ideal of physical virginity goes the concept of a mental 'purity' which would be sullied by any knowledge of sex. Female students cannot risk being heard discussing sex, because they are just as vulnerable as other Palestinian women to gossip. For many of them, their relative freedom at university is strictly provisional. If a rumour of immodest behaviour – and this would include too much curiosity about sex – were to reach their parents, they would be withdrawn and returned to strict supervision. I asked Fadwa why the committee planned lectures rather than small group discussions. She explained:

> No one would dare open her mouth. There is great resistance in our culture to the idea of telling anyone your problems. You have to assume that whatever you confess will immediately be spread all over the community and used to discredit and dishonour you.

A fundamental demand is for women to be acknowledged as active sexual beings, instead of just the objects of men's reproductive urge. The idea is not entirely new: the *Koran*, some medieval Islamic writers, and peasant tradition do accept women's active sexuality to a certain degree. But it seems that this tradition has been overlaid by a 'Victorian' idea of women as passive and passionless beings. When marriage partners were in a contractual relationship in which the power structure echoed the father-daughter relationship and the age difference between them was often fifteen or twenty years or more, the idea could be sustained that women were sexually passive beings without rights. Now that marriage is becoming a voluntary relationship in which partners are increasingly likely to be close in age and have equal access to wealth, women's supposed sexual passivity is being challenged. During Salwa's period in prison, sexuality was one of the serious topics of discussion:

> We talked a lot about relationships, and about how our bodies work . . . We got used to the idea that sex is a subject that can be discussed, just as politics is. We stopped feeling ashamed, and we were in a situation where we trusted one another completely so we could say anything. That situation never exists outside prison . . . Normally even a husband and wife can't talk about sex, especially village people. You often hear women say sex isn't important, or even that they hate it. Maybe they were frightened the first time because they didn't know that sex can be a pleasure and part of a relationship. They think it's something that men just do to women – the woman opens her legs and the man enjoys himself. If women like this see a girl enjoying sex on television, they say, 'Look how terrible, she's nothing but a whore'. Maybe they just say that to make a good impression on their husband and children; I think in their hearts they're thinking, 'I wish I could experience something like that, I wish my husband and I felt like that together'. But it would be shameful to admit that's what they're thinking . . . There shouldn't be any shame between a husband and wife. Women should be able to take the initiative sometimes, ask their husbands to sleep with them, refuse them when they don't feel like it. I think now some educated women are learning how to do this. They get married older, and know each other first, and they're able to discuss things.

The undying family

That women have the right to know their bodies, that they have an equal right with men to sexual pleasure: such ideas echo the growth of women's self-consciousness and self-confidence in the West. The logical outcome should be the assertion of absolute equality and freedom from domination by men. But such a radical position is not on the agenda of Palestinian women, at least not at the level of public debate. Seeking improvement in their social position, women are working for a general rise in their status, and relaxation of men's hold over them, and for various specific freedoms. What they do not seem to be doing widely is analysing the underlying causes of women's subordination – which they would find, if they searched, in the institution of the family as it is conceived at present.

It is in order to perpetuate the patriarchal family that men have controlled women's reproductivity, and consequently their minds, movements and labour. Palestinian women appear on the whole to share their society's conviction that the family is a sacred, natural, and fundamentally unquestionable institution. (I do not mean to imply that families are not desirable, but to point out that Palestinians, like many people nowadays in the West, are ignoring the dangers to women's equality inherent in an uncritical, sentimental, ideological acceptance of the 'traditional family'.) 'The Family' is regarded approvingly as one of the salient and best characteristics of Arab and Islamic culture. Even Marxist political views can coexist with an unwillingness to analyse the family in economic terms. Changes in the size and function of the family in recent decades, for instance, are not acknowledged. It is not only Muslim revivalists who condemn the 'collapse of the family' in the West and see it as caused by a vaguely defined moral degeneration, unconnected with economic changes. Most women appear to acquiesce surprisingly in their society's sexual morality deriving from the stucture of the family, with its double standard which requires chastity of women but not of men. Its crueller and most unreasonable manifestations are condemned, but its fundamental premises not questioned.

Several reasons can be found why Palestinian women have not made the logical step towards dissecting the family ideal. One is simply that the movement towards liberation is still at an early stage of its history, and for the majority of women it is enough for the time being to work for immediate practical freedoms, without worrying about analysing the whole system of gender and power relations, an analysis which must seem at best academic. There are powerful tactical reasons, too, for avoiding analysis. Challenges to the system would alienate both men and the majority of women, and certainly not help women in their practical struggle for greater freedom. As in other similar situations (such as nineteenth-century Britain), women have to be careful not to offend their society's strictest standards of propriety and morality. Perceived 'immorality' could be expected to provoke a backlash of conservatism and jeopardise every gain made so far. Any suspicion that women's groups were questioning the institution of the family would produce widespread hostility.

The impossibility of raising certain questions publicly probably stifles debate and hinders the spread of new ideas. Another impediment is nationalism. As we have already seen, the struggle for national liberation is a powerful impetus for women to seek their own freedom. At the same time, overriding as it does every other issue, the national cause acts as a brake on addressing properly the question of women's social position. This happens in two ways. First, there is the problem, familiar all over the world, that politics is seen as separate from everyday life. A woman can gain the freedom to participate in political or even military activity and be accepted as an equal partner by men, without this having any effect on her position in everyday social life. She is being accepted as an honorary man, and her social position as a woman is not implicated or addressed. Women's success in the 'man's world' indeed distracts attention from and disguises their lack of progress socially. Salwa experienced this herself:

> There was a huge gap between my political and my social development. Within my *feda'i* group, there were no degrees of higher or lower, man or woman, and we felt equal. I could go to work with a man with my head held high. But as soon as we got back into society, the barrier went up again. With my comrades I could discuss things as if I was a man, but at home I went on bowing to my father. I never thought, 'I'm a strong person, why should I obey him?' If my father said, 'Don't go out', I stayed at home. If I had to meet a comrade in the street, just to exchange a simple message like 'Tomorrow, OK?', I'd come home trembling in case someone told my father they'd seen me talking to a strange man . . . And when you are arrested, your first thought is not, 'O God, how can I face interrogation and torture!' It is, 'What will my father do to me?'

Men do not recognise this phenomenon, Salwa says:

> Men talk a great deal about the equality of women, and they truly believe that they have allowed women to become equal . . . They see women

taking part in the national struggle, going on strike, going to prison. They see that women are not hidden and oppressed as they were in the past, and they believe that everything is already achieved. But at home, and in personal relationships, there is no equality.

Because the national struggle has priority, Palestinian women also tend to dismiss concern with personal relationships – beyond the bare minimum necessary for activity – as irrelevant and distracting. Demands for sexual and gender equality are dismissively referred to as 'feminism', and regarded as a luxury to be indulged in by the spoiled bourgeoisie of the rich West. As a result, even politically active and progressive women are often paradoxically conservative in their views on sex and gender. Fadwa, for all her support for the Communist Party and reforming zeal to spread sex education among students, is thoroughly romantic and uncritical:

> If my husband slept with another woman, I would forgive him and try to win back his love – that's woman's nature, isn't it? But if I slept with someone else – no, I wouldn't expect him to forgive me.

Salwa also revealed her failure to question the fundamentals of sexual power relations when she told me the story of some Palestinian women prisoners who were raped by Israeli prison guards in 1968. Traditionally, as we have seen from Salwa's earlier story, rape was blamed on the victim and regarded as the greatest possible dishonour to her family, so women who had been raped would keep it secret, from a powerful combination of fear and shame. These women prisoners dared to defy shame and announce in court that they had been raped. In doing this they were dealing a blow against one of the Israelis' most effective weapons against Palestinians, the threat of raping Palestinian women. They became national heroines (and still are, twenty years later – several women told me the story). But to Western eyes their stand does not seem to have been very radical. Their plea, at least as Salwa reported it to me, was that non-virginity should be forgiven when it results from enemy action. They did not attempt to claim that virginity is a woman's private affair.

It is easy to understand why Palestinian women have not launched a full-frontal attack on patriarchy. However, the lack of a theoretical basis for their social aspirations creates many paradoxes for individual women and perhaps weakens the force of the women's movement as a whole. Without the arguments to understand and explain their constraints, women have less conviction, less confidence, and less power to act freely even in pursuit of their most moderate and practicable demands. As an example, Salwa herself is caught in a family situation which she could probably endure better or even solve if she analysed it more clearly. Although she was a *feda'iye* and spent seven years suffering and resisting in gaol, she is now, unmarried and in her mid-twenties, living at home, where her very traditional father keeps watch over her movements and social contacts. She says ruefully:

> I would have more freedom if I were married, but who can I marry? It has to be a Christian. Though my parents are very open-minded about most things, and supported me wonderfully all through prison, my father would cut me off completely if I married a Muslim. And I have no right to hurt him so after he has been so good to me all my life. The problem is, all the men I have met who I think I could be happy with, who share my political interests and have been through the same suffering as I have, are Muslims.

To Salwa, her situation seems quite unchangeable and hopeless. Despite her progressive analysis of sexual relations, she does not push analysis so far as to criticise the power structure of the family and ask by what right her father has authority over her.

It hardly need be said that obedience to the strict norms of the family ideal is not total. Many individual women are successfully challenging expectations in their thoughts and in their behaviour, quietly and without creating scandals. A few are defying the woman-as-mother image by deciding not to have children. Some have husbands who share the housework and childcare with them. Some are their husbands' professional equals, working as hard and earning as much. A few are living alone; some are managing to find the privacy for extra-marital sexual relationships. None of these stands is easy, and they can only be made, on the whole, by the most educated professional women, whose economic independence allows them to rule themselves, and whose standing to some extent fends off criticism of their personal 'character'.

6

Education

Some analysts of women's progress worldwide suggest that education is the single most important factor in improving women's lives and status. Certainly it correlates with improvements in family health and standards of living, and in women's personal independence and access to wealth. Palestinians tend to argue that it is increasing wealth rather than education which is the leading factor in improving women's lot. They believe that the education of women should be seen as one of many positive results of escape from the pressures of the subsistence economy. Whichever view one takes, it is clear that education is one of the most visible and far-reaching of the changes Palestinian women are experiencing.

The change has been rapid and widespread. Fifty years ago, the majority of Palestinians saw no value in education for women. All the rural women over the age of fifty whom I interviewed were illiterate or had learned to read recently in literacy classes. In many of their families, daughters in their mid twenties who had received only two or three years of schooling were now watching their sisters ten years younger studying hard and discussing which college to go to when they had passed their exams.

The growth of education

Women's move into education has been part of a dramatic expansion in education for all Palestinians, which grew slowly through the first half of the twentieth century and rapidly after 1948. At the beginning of the century, schooling was available in Islamic schools (for boys) and in European and American mission schools (for girls as well). These schools were mostly situated in towns and served the elite. For the majority of the rural population education was inaccessible. The Ottoman government passed laws making elementary schooling compulsory for both sexes, but the small number of schools it built fell far short of actually providing for everyone. The British mandate government did not do a great deal to improve the situation, although by then demand was increasing as Palestinians began to realise the role education must play in helping them to survive in a fast-changing and threatening world. British officials visiting villages were reportedly surrounded by women clamouring 'Give us schools!'. By the end of the mandate, only one-third of Arab school-age children were in school, of whom one-fifth were girls (while the Jewish community, which ran its own schools instead of depending on the British government, was managing to educate nearly 100 per cent of its children).

After 1948 the need for education became more urgent. Palestinians often say 'We lost our country in 1948 because the Zionists were educated and we were not'. They see education as a political weapon and want to catch up and confront Israel on equal terms. Less heroically, the demand for education is explicable as a matter of economic survival. 'Our wealth used to be our land. When that was taken away from us, we turned to education.' The United Nations Relief and Works Agency (UNRWA) saw the provision of education as one of its primary duties from the beginning and established schooling up to the age of fourteen for all refugees, as well as centres for vocational and teacher training. UNRWA made a particular point of providing the same level of school facilities for girls as for boys.

For those who did not lose their land in 1948 the transformation from a peasant to a wage-earning economy meant that land became a less secure form of wealth, while education became correspondingly more attractive. Villagers say simply, 'Education is money'. The particular situation of Palestine from the 1950s onwards made the benefits of education starkly clear: in contrast to the stagnant economy and hardships of life as a labourer at home glittered the wealth of the many Palestinians who, with education to help them, emigrated to become the professional and administrative backbone of the newly-developing Gulf oil states or prosperous merchants in the United States or Central America. During the 1950s and 1960s the Jordanian government built many new schools in towns and rural areas in the West Bank to meet the growing demand.

When Israel occupied the West Bank and Gaza Strip in 1967, the responsibilities it took on included administration of the schools previously run by the Jordanian and Egyptian governments. The school population has continued to grow, with an increase in the population and an increasing demand for education. Today, government schools account for around 78 per cent of school students in the occupied territories, while 14 per cent attend UNRWA schools and 8 per cent are in the private sector.

Almost all children of both sexes attend at least primary school, and the belief that education is necessary is nearly universal. What proportion continue through secondary school is not precisely known, as Palestinians are not allowed to collect statistics, and the Israeli authorities do not release them (having no interest in allowing comparisons to be made between Palestinian schooling under occupation and education in Israel or other countries). It seems that roughly equal numbers of boys and girls drop out of school after the age of twelve or so – boys to seek work, girls for traditional social and domestic reasons. Israeli official statistics say that only 30 per cent of Palestinian pupils graduate from secondary school. It can be supposed that Israel has an interest in minimising educational achievements of Palestinians; Palestinian teachers, with the opposite interest, put the figure considerably higher.

At the tertiary stage, provision of vocational and teacher training in the occupied territories is inadequate, but Palestinians are renowned for having one of the highest rates of university graduates of any nation in the world. (Israeli soldiers expressed patronising wonder when they found the works of Marx and Lenin in the abandoned positions of Palestinian fighters in Lebanon in 1982: this only shows how little Israelis know, or care to know, about the people they have displaced.)

The 1980s have seen a slight hesitation in the onward march of education. The end of the golden age of opportunity for Palestinians in the Gulf coincided with a recession in the Israeli economy. Unemployment has brought disillusionment, and it seems that more young people are dropping out of school to look for work earlier as the economic benefits of education look less certain. It is not clear whether this is true for girls as well as boys. Their commitment to education has never been so closely tied to the economic situation, as fewer of them work. At the same time, the gains education brings them in terms of personal status and freedom are unquestionable.

Women's move into education

The mass move of women into education came later than men's because of the strong economic and cultural pressures against it. As in many other societies, education was traditionally not thought necessary or desirable for girls: not necessary, because of women's position in the economic structure of the family – women did not earn income, and their unpaid domestic labour (for which education might render them unfit) was essential for the family's survival; not desirable, because it was seen as threatening male honour and male position in the social hierarchy. Fathers used to oppose education on the grounds that it led to immorality – 'I'll not have my daughter going to school so that she can write her own love-letters!' – and it was associated with freedom of thought and independence.

In the 1950s and 1960s, especially in rural areas, custom, poor transport, poverty and the lack of jobs to justify education kept most girls at home. The past two decades have witnessed a profound shift in attitudes: girls now form 40 per cent of pupils in secondary as well as primary schools, and even in traditional villages a high-school education is a desirable attribute in a wife.

Rising expectations and the availability of jobs mean that women's earning power is increasingly valued, but the connection between economic opportunity and education does not seem to be a simple one. Most of the jobs available to women, in Israeli agriculture and factories, are unskilled and would hardly require literacy. Perhaps the explanation for this contradiction lies in men's greater willingness to trust educated women to leave the protection of home.

The pressures and insecurities of occupation are seen as another force behind the change. The uncertainty of the future makes it desirable for girls as well as boys to be equipped to support themselves and deal with yet-unknown problems. Politics too claims its role: 'Women are half the nation, and we can't afford to leave them useless; we must develop all our nation's potential'.

Girls' struggles for the right to education

Women have come a long way, and the influence of what they have gained has far-reaching effects on their lives, but they do not yet have equal and automatic access to education. Indeed, in how many societies do they? The tradition of excluding them was so fundamental to the social order that it will take generations to disappear. For one thing, the economic facts of marriage still argue against giving girls' education equal priority with boys'. Whereas investing money in a son's education brings its reward in a higher-paid and higher-status job which will benefit the parents in their dependent old age, money spent on a girl's education is money lost, as it is still widely expected that she will not work once she is married, and any income she does earn will go to the family she marries into, not her own. Honour too is a value still upheld, especially in rural communities, and still measured according to traditional behaviour and relationships. Many traditional and less educated men see the education and 'modern' behaviour of their daughters as undermining their authority over the family and their position in the community.

The following stories are typical of the thousands of individual conflicts between generations and sexes within families through which girls have asserted their newly-perceived rights and taken an important step towards independence.

Zeinab was born in 1960 in a village in the centre of the West Bank not far away from Birzeit University. Her father has a job in a bus depot in Israel and lives away from home during the week. Working in Israel and leaving his family unprotected constitute a double threat to his honour and self-esteem. He has tried to compensate by exerting stern control over his wife and daughters. Zeinab, from her early teens, saw education as not just her personal right but a national duty. Though her father had been active in the national movement in his youth, he was not happy that his daughter should involve herself in the dangers and exposure of public and political life. He was bewildered by Zeinab's desire for independence and her determination to leave the tried and trusted world of the village. Her demands were an unacceptable challenge to his authority and dignity, to which his response at first was irrational brutality.

The first obstacles Zeinab had to deal with were the domestic demands made on her:

> I got a low grade when I first took *Tawjihi* [the high-school graduation exam] because our conditions at home were so bad. We didn't have

running water or electricity in the village, and we hadn't yet built our well at home, so I had to work very hard. School finished at three o'clock, I walked the three kilometres home, then I had to go down to the spring, two kilometres away, to fetch water. Then I had to get up at four in the morning to go down again. Sometimes we borrowed my grandfather's donkey, but if we had quarrelled with him, which often happened, I had to carry the water myself. By the evening, I was too tired to study.

Then she came up against her father's efforts to impose his ideal of a good daughter on her:

I thought I would repeat the year at school and try again, but my father refused to let me. He said, 'You've had your chance, and that's it, finished. I've got your brothers to educate now. Either get married, or at least stay at home and help your mother, she needs you.' He wanted me to marry a cousin whom I knew and didn't like. I refused because I knew it would be the end of my progress if I married him. My father accepted my decision not to marry yet, but he wouldn't let me go back to school. He was afraid that if I were educated I would go away and leave the family. Even now he fears that. Last time we had a row he accused me, 'It's just as I thought, you are leaving us, wanting independence'. He wants to keep me 'under his hand', of course, that's how men are.

During a short and itself hard-won period spent working under the protection of her aunt in a local pharmaceutical factory, and then teaching a literacy class in the village in the afternoons, Zeinab saved some money. Without consulting her parents she enrolled herself in a secretarial course at the vocational college in the town ten kilometres away. The next stage was a job in a bookshop:

By now my parents accepted that I couldn't sit at home and would never be content unless I was working. Each new step I take, they oppose it for a month or so, and then when I insist they get used to it.

Her plan was to study at home and re-sit the school-leaving exam so that she could apply for university. When her father found out about this ambition, his opposition flared up again.

The trouble was, there was no precedent that he knew of a village girl going away to university and becoming an independent professional person. The only professional woman he had ever met was from a bourgeois background. He could accept that different standards applied to her, but he couldn't accept them in his own family. He kept me at home like a prisoner. He took away all my money, thinking that would stop me from doing anything by myself. The fee for the exam was about three dinars [£6] – not much, but a lot if you don't have it. The last day before registration for the exam closed, a friend came and found me sitting here crying. 'What's the matter?' When I explained, she said, 'My fiancé has given me some money; take it'. She went down to the fields and kept my mother talking, and I ran to the next village and got a bus into town to enrol.

Now Zeinab tried to settle down to study seriously.

More problems. I couldn't tell my mother, because she was afraid of my father and agreed with all his opinions. To stop her suspecting anything I was embroidering her a dress, and that took a lot of my time. I couldn't study during the day, I had to do it all after midnight, after the village generator had been switched off. My father found out anyway. He came bursting into the room where I was studying one night. He hit me and threatened to burn my books. 'Do whatever you want', I said. 'You can't stop me now. I'll just buy the books again.'

Finally Zeinab won a scholarship to the university, where she studied hard and successfully. By the time she graduated her parents were proud of her. So completely had they been won round to the idea of education that they were anxious for her sister to follow in her footsteps, and now deny they ever opposed Zeinab. Her mother says,

I want my girls to have a different life from mine. They mustn't be stuck in the house like I was, with no education.

Not everyone has the self-confidence and determination of Zeinab. Faika, a younger girl in the same village, could not sustain her vaguer ambitions in the face of her family's hostility and her own lack of a role model. Her story is an extreme but not unique example of how even today, in families where education is highly valued for boys, girls may be disregarded and kept in exploitable ignorance.

My parents took me away from school when I was nine. The teacher said I wasn't very bright and they might as well take me away. My father was ill, and we had to find money for my brothers to go to university, so I stayed at home to look after the house while my mother went out to work as a cleaner. For five years I hardly left the village. We had no electricity then, no television, nothing. Most of my friends were going to school, but I didn't really mind, I didn't know what was good for me.

At fourteen, Faika tried to go back to school. She was supported by Zeinab, who persuaded Faika's parents to allow her to attend the adult literacy class, then persuaded the headmistress of the local school to accept Faika. Faika continues:

> Four days after I started back at school, my family sent me away to Jordan to work as a servant in the house of some cousins. One of my brothers was at university, the other was about to start at a college where he had to pay high fees. I spent two miserable years there. The family treated me badly, especially the children my own age. They shouted and said I was stupid. I was determined to prove they were wrong, and I decided I wanted to become a doctor.

So Faika begged her mother to let her come home, and tried once more to take up her studies. For the first year all went well, but her family was persistently hostile. Her brothers, both now at home and unemployed, would not let her work to earn herself pocket money and prevented her from seeing Zeinab, whom they regarded as a bad influence. In this environment her goal seemed distant, and her confidence was further undermined by the sexual and social frustration of an adult woman forced to live and study among children. Her enthusiasm collapsed in disillusionment and depression.

> How can I carry on studying, when we have no money? I worked to pay for my brothers' education, but I don't expect them to pay for mine. I'll just go and work in the factory, or look for a husband. I'm so tired, everything's a problem.

The school system

The narrowly academic content and rigid methods of school education do nothing to make it easier for pupils like Faika who need to develop confidence in themselves. Nor does the system contribute very positively to Palestinian national development. Highly committed as they are to education as a means of individual and national liberation, Palestinians would probably devote considerable material and intellectual resources to developing their own school system if they had the opportunity. As it is, they have very little control over what they teach and how. Private and

UNRWA schools have a degree of autonomy, limited by the occupation's censorship laws, the economic environment, and the need to follow the inherited curricula of Jordan and Egypt. But government schools are under the direct control of the Israeli military government, which through a combination of severe underfunding and close political control ensures that the Palestinian staff and pupils have no freedom to adapt the system to their needs. Hala, a Ramallah teacher, expresses the frustration of working in a system which she thinks pernicious but cannot change:

> In the 1950s the Jordanian regime established a school system that supported its interests – and Jordan is a conservative and illiberal state. In 1967, the Israelis took over the system and they run it in the way that best suits them. How can it be good for us Palestinians? Nobody has ever cared about what we need.

Hala feels that the curriculum hinders rather than helps the Palestinian people's effort to take responsibility for their fate and prepare themselves for personal and political liberation. With its perspective limited to achievement in academic exams, the curriculum encourages

> a method of teaching that is even more repressive than the content of the courses themselves. It's just rote learning, listening to the teacher and repeating what he or she says. No questioning, no creativity or imagination. It teaches pupils not to think for themselves.

Like inherited colonial systems in other countries, the education system in the occupied territories teaches individualism and elitism. Hala feels that the harmful social effects are incalculable.

> It perpetuates all the worst features of Palestinian society. The pupils don't learn co-operation, they learn competition. Successful students absorb the idea that they are entitled to money, good jobs, privilege; the unacademic ones feel like failures. It's socially and politically divisive, exactly what we don't need for our struggle. And it's quite inappropriate to the real labour needs of the country.

How much can such a system contribute to changing the social position of women and helping them develop confidence in themselves?

Success at school does give girls self-respect, and wins them the respect of men. But I believe that working and earning money are more powerful factors, and apart from giving girls the means to do that better, schools are not otherwise liberating. They are single-sex, for one thing. There's no time allowed for discussing social questions and issues of importance for women. The Israeli authorities would probably think such subjects were political incitement anyway, and ban them. Even traditional girls' subjects like Home Economics, which can be very important in raising consciousness and promoting self-reliance, are badly taught because of the lack of qualified teachers and facilities.

Underfunding is chronic in government schools. No new schools have been built since 1967. Many existing schools are not purpose-built and all suffer from a shortage of classrooms; many work a double-shift system, and even so classes are large, reinforcing the rigidity of the teaching style. Heating and sanitary facilities are primitive, and extras like art and craft rooms and sports facilities rare. More than half the schools in the West Bank have no library and no laboratory, with girls' schools faring worse than boys' in this respect.

Teaching contains a large proportion of professional working women. Here, as in other countries, teaching has for many years been a convenient and socially acceptable job for women, so women bear their share of the difficulties and unpleasantness of teaching:

Teaching is a terrible job. We are demoralised and stressed. The physical conditions are bad enough, but the psychological conditions are worse. You work very hard, for very low pay, in constant fear of the authorities, who punish you if they think you're the least bit subversive.

Hala knows what the punishments are. For her own involvement in attempts to set up a trade union for teachers in government schools, she has had pay increments withheld, and been demoted. The last time I met her, she was expecting to receive an order to transfer to a school that was one and a half hour's journey from her home. The authorities fear the potential power of teachers to influence a very large part of the Palestinian population; by measures such as these they attempt to obstruct and intimidate them.

Political flashpoints

Not discouraged by the repressive environment and authoritarian content of their studies, school students, girls as well as boys, more than any other sector of Palestinian society have been volatile and active in their opposition to the occupation. They attracted international attention for the fearless persistence of their defiance during the *intifada*, but the role was not new to them. Students are a large body and easy to organise, and their power to cause disturbance and perhaps spark off demonstrations among their more cautious elders is considerable. The authorities therefore keep a strict watch. They maintain a permanent effort to crush the students' spirit through the punishing conditions of schooling, censorship of textbooks, and banning of discussion of national history, culture and political issues. Military responses to demonstrations and targeted centres of activity are harsh. Soldiers invade schools and intimidate younger as well as more senior pupils. Schools have been closed for periods from a few days to months to prevent or punish protests. Students identified as leaders are regularly punished by being imprisoned for a few days (without charge or trial) over the end-of-year exam period so that they cannot graduate. Teachers suspected of encouraging them are punished.

A young teacher in Hebron described the dilemmas teachers often find themselves in:

> There are lots of national celebrations and commemoration days – Balfour Declaration Day, Land Day, the first action of Fatah. On those days the students come into school but they don't want to study maths or writing. They ask you 'What is this celebration? What does it mean? What happened?' The teacher struggles in her mind; she wants to answer them frankly, but at the same time she is afraid that some collaborator will report her to the authorities. (Plenty of school heads collaborate – anyone who showed a spark of resistance would not be promoted to the position.) The teacher suffers if she doesn't help the students understand their national history, and she may suffer if she does.
>
> After the Camp David accords, there were protest demonstrations all over the occupied territories, and the military government closed all the schools and accused lots of teachers of inciting disturbances. I was vulnerable because I was a geography teacher, and geography is a very sensitive subject. If you have an old map with the name Palestine on it, for instance, you have to paint it out and put in 'Israel' instead. My

headmistress accused me of ' wasting time on unimportant subjects and neglecting the course work'. She reported me to the military government education department, and I was transferred from the secondary school where I was working to a primary school in a village several miles away. They think you will make less trouble in a primary school because the girls are too young and unaware to ask any questions. I have no prospect of being promoted now, of course, because I am black-listed. Not that I mind that: who would want to be promoted in our present condition? While if we had a state of our own, I would be happy to be the door-keeper.

Higher education

In the field of further education, Palestinians have greater freedom to set their own goals and standards. There are some Israeli government training centres, but most of the provision is by local private and charitable institutions, which are not subject to the same degrees of control by the Israeli authorities or the Jordanian educational system. Despite its relative freedom, the tertiary sector does have many problems, some due directly to the occupation, some due rather to the very independence and haphazard growth of the institutions themselves, and to the absence of any effective national education planning body.

The occupied territories are understandably proud of their universities. The first to open its doors for four-year undergraduate degree courses was Birzeit, in the West Bank, in 1972. Since then three others have been established in the West Bank and one in Gaza – Bethlehem, Najah in Nablus, Hebron, and the Islamic University of Gaza. Between them in 1982–3 they were educating around 10,000 students, of whom over 40 per cent were women. Though they are private institutions, they receive funding from various Arab sources outside and are able to keep their fees low; the social catchment area of their students is fairly wide.

The universities are a source of pride not only for their educational role, which is valued both for its prestige and for its perceived contribution to national development, but also because they are among the few Palestinian national institutions in the occupied territories. They take their national responsibilities seriously, determinedly maintaining their independence from Israeli control and trying to focus their curricula on national needs.

At Bethlehem University courses are geared towards services such as nursing and local economic activity, particularly the hotel trade. At Birzeit, all students are required to undertake a certain amount of community work in building programmes, social service or helping with harvests. Several universities have established research departments to investigate and develop archives of Palestinian history, sociology and economy. Birzeit has extra-mural departments doing practical work in literacy and public health.

The national role of the universities certainly increases their vitality and at times their influence, but it also exacerbates the enormous difficulties of running a relevant and creative education system under occupation. The Israeli authorities fear the political power of the universities. In the face of protests from the Israeli and international academic community, the government stopped short of imposing a military order – number 854 – which would have brought universities under the same direct control as it exercises over schools. Instead they exert constant pressure in other ways: the refusal of building permits, heavy taxation and the obstruction of funding, censorship and the unavailability of books, the occasional expulsion of staff, frequent closure, the harassment of students. In this situation of constant confrontation, it is hard for university administrations to balance the students' demands for political expression with the danger of provoking Israeli reprisals. The universities have had internal political problems too, reflecting the troubled relationships of the PLO internally and with Arab states, and the rise of Islamic fundamentalism. Maintaining independence from funders, trying to satisfy student political demands, and containing student political rivalries, have at times virtually paralysed some of the universities.

Another contentious area is the question of balancing the priority of academic standards with the duty to extend education as widely as possible. There is also the fundamental problem of what to teach. It is not at all easy to define what the role of a university should be in an economic situation such as the West Bank and Gaza Strip face. Should universities concentrate on training which will enable graduates to earn their living abroad? This was the option chosen in the early years, and prestigious engineering departments were established to train graduates to work in the Gulf. With recession and fewer opportunities for emigration, this focus is being increasingly questioned. On the other hand, how can universities maintain their dynamism when planning for the future means preparing graduates who will be useful in a future self-governing independent state but who are for the time being unemployable? The Israeli economy will not, and the occupied territories cannot, absorb many Palestinian graduates, and this is a problem the universities collectively and students individually have not been able to resolve.

Women are well-represented in the Palestinian universities. However, the appearance of equality is deceptive: many families who can afford to have chosen to send their sons abroad for their university education, but relatively few are prepared to invest so much money in their daughters or allow them so far out of their sight. Overall, women are still fewer than men in undergraduate and graduate studies – they are still restricted by the view that the income and status of their job will be less important than that of their husband. Nonetheless, women's presence in higher education is significant given how rare it was a generation ago. The establishment of local universities did present women with new opportunities which they have not hesitated to take advantage of, and they are perhaps less segregated into specific 'girls'' subjects than in many European countries. The highest proportion of women students, 55 per cent in 1981–2, was at the University of Hebron, which only offers courses in arts and Islamic subjects. Women do not enter courses of technical training for traditionally men's jobs, but they are well represented in sciences, forming, for example, nearly 30 per cent of the engineering school at Birzeit University. One of the paradoxes of Palestinian society in the recent past has been that, though women are still not treated as responsible adults with regard to their own sexuality, in professional life they face relatively little gender discrimination. Elevated above everyday concerns and, as it were, desexualised by the high regard Palestinians have for the professions, women work successfully as doctors, lawyers, architects and academics.

For the majority of women university students I knew in the years 1981–5, reaching university had been the goal sustaining them through their schooldays. It was only towards the end of their courses that some of them began to define career ambitions and perceive the difficulties of finding the opportunities and the social freedom to fulfil them. The expectation is still that women will marry, and that if they work at all they will regard their job as less important than their position at home. Many women students share this expectation, but even many of those who do not are unable to find work, because of the social pressure to remain living at home and the shortage of acceptable jobs. For them, readjustment to the constraints of home life is hard and disillusioning. (For men graduates, too, unemployment is a serious problem, but they do not face the same social restrictions as women.) What women gain from university is the pleasure and status of education for its own sake, the opportunity to prove equal capability with men, and, for those studying away from home, the experience of a social freedom not available anywhere else in Palestinian society. In all these respects university is a separate world, isolated from real life. Pushing the Palestinian society and economy to accept and value fully its educated women remains a challenge.

Other further education

Vocational and technical training are less developed than universities, though here too there is growing awareness of the need to co-ordinate planning and develop courses relevant to the nation's needs. A technical and scientific college, UNRWA vocational colleges for refugees, two small agricultural colleges, some nursing colleges, professional training in such fields as social work and kindergarten teaching, and some private and charitable secretarial training institutions, are all well-established and responding with varying degrees of flexibility to new pressures and new debates. One of the reasons less attention has been paid to this sector than to universities is the lack of prestige Palestinians accord technical education compared with academic. Thus there has been little incentive to set up private institutions to provide it. Demand for technical education is not high, partly influenced by the very low priority given to practical subjects in schools. Overall, of course, there is the problem of the stagnant economy of the occupied territories, which offers young people little incentive to train.

Informal education

Education for adults outside the structure of schools and colleges had been the focus of great interest and activity. Instigated and controlled by local Palestinian voluntary organisations, education was part of the mid–1970s commitment to mobilise the occupied territories population, and later of the desire to develop appropriate and self-reliant services. Women are the main beneficiaries of informal education, which is often aimed at compensating for their disadvantaged access to formal education and limited social contacts, and in particular at helping them earn money and manage their domestic responsibilities better. Voluntary organisations hold literacy and vocational classes in villages and camps, and provide vocational training in areas relevant to women, such as literacy teaching, kindergarten teaching, and community health work.

The informal sector can be more flexible and more responsive to changing needs than institutional education. It requires much smaller financial investment, relies on the commitment and enthusiasm of its activists, is closer to the people it serves, and is not constrained by externally imposed goals and standards. As yet the achievements are limited. The lack of co-ordination among different organisations exacerbates the problems of lack of resources and experience and lack of overall structure. Good ideas and good intentions are sometimes not followed through or spread widely. The principal value of many classes is that they mobilise people and provide a social and generally educational activity for village women who lack stimulation and opportunities to leave home.

Many of the problems that informal education hopes to tackle are really beyond the scope of any voluntary groups. A lot of goodwill and words have been spent on the question of vocational training for women. The economic context offers so few opportunities that it is hardly surprising if successful training projects are the exception rather than the rule. The skills most widely taught, partly because they are culturally acceptable and partly because they require little investment, have been dress-making, embroidery and knitting. How many women can really earn their living with these skills? They have been taught by all women's organisations, offered automatically and taken up by the women students because they are relatively useful skills and there are no other options, but little attention has been given to whether, or how, they could be made economically useful. The problems of looking for real economic possibilities within the constraints of women's social restrictions and the Israeli-dominated economy, and of mastering skills needed to make them succeed, are only now being addressed, boosted like so many other areas of development by the *intifada*.

New ideas in education

The *intifada* also showed how ready Palestinians are for new thinking in formal education. For a whole academic year from December 1987, all schools in the West Bank were closed by military order. Concern about the social and educational effects on children of a year without school led some of the newly-established neighbourhood committees to set up alternative education programmes. Classes were held in homes, with students, professional teachers, and anyone with relevant skills drafted in as volunteer teachers. Operating entirely clandestinely, outside the reach of the Israeli military or the Jordanian education system, the classes had a freedom unprecedented in Palestinian educational experience. They were welcomed, in educational circles at least, as an opportunity for pupils and teachers together to develop new approaches to schooling. Predictably, the practice was not so exciting as the theory, and the greatest immediate impact of the neighbourhood schools was in raising morale. But they had more lasting effects too. Education professionals focused on developing pupil-centred teaching materials, many teachers were brought face to face with new ideas, and the experiment generated a level of enthusiasm in the community at large which will have sown the seeds of new ideas in education for the future.

7

Agricultural work

Palestinian women have always worked. The image beloved of Western orientalists, of Arab women veiled, secluded and unproductive, may once have been a fair reflection of the lives of the women of Palestine's leisured urban upper class, but it was never representative of the hard-working rural majority. Peasant women work the land, tend animals, supply the material and social needs of their households. Their work is both productive and reproductive: in a subsistence farming economy the two are hardly distinct. But work in itself, even productive work, does not accord the worker high status and independence. Power follows from control of the means and products of labour, which Palestinian women have not had. According to Islamic law, women can own property and run businesses, but in practice it has been rare for them to be the managers of their own production. In a society organised into patriarchal tribal and extended family units, women's productive and reproductive functions are appropriated for the prosperity of families, and are controlled by men.

Rural self-sufficiency before 1967

By the beginning of the twentieth century, agriculture in Palestine was fairly thoroughly incorporated into the world market system, with citrus plantations on the coast and large estates in the fertile inland valleys producing for export. Capitalism had not taken hold everywhere, however. In the hill country the West Bank, peasants continued to farm their smallholdings largely for their own

97

subsistence. In some more remote areas this way of life continued through the 1950s and early 1960s, with very little money entering the local economy until the occupation drew men away to wage labour in Israel. The region of Yatta in the south of the West Bank was one such area. Umm Issa describes the essential role played by women in the economic life of her largely self-sufficient community before 1967:

I'd start early in the morning with milking my three cows, then I'd make bread, then I'd carry my baby down to my father's fields and work there. At the end of the afternoon I came back, cleaned the house, looked after the children and cooked. Then I milked the cows again, made butter if it was the season, laid out my bed and slept. We spent most of our time outside. In Jordanian times we used to sleep in the fields during the planting and harvesting season. We felt safe then; since the occupation, we've been afraid, so we come and go every day . . . We didn't have any time to sit doing embroidery, except in the summer after the harvest was over; anyway we couldn't have afforded to make ourselves new clothes all the time. Most women had just two or three *thoobs* [dresses] and men had one. For work in the fields, we wore our old worn-out clothes, patched with sixty patches! The men's *thoobs* got very dirty. I'd take my husband's to the well and wash it with soap and a stone and hang it to dry, and it would be ready for him the next morning. Meanwhile he had to lie in bed with nothing on. Nobody had more clothes than anyone else, we were all living at the same level.

We used to go to Hebron for shopping rather than the village shops, as we thought things were cheaper there. I don't know how long it took to walk there, we didn't know about time. We didn't have to buy much, because almost everything we needed came from our land: barley, corn, lentils, cucumbers, melons and watermelons, vegetables. We ate bread and noodles made from our own wheat, not imported rice like we do now. You could sometimes buy a little rice from the market if you needed it. We had cows and used the milk or butter or yoghurt for cooking. Ours is not an olive-tree area, and only four or five families in the village had olives. If we needed olive oil for some special purpose like treating an illness, we had to buy a little bottle. Kerosene for lighting we had to buy, three kilos a year. A little sugar, but we didn't have tea so we didn't use nearly as much as we do now. We drank coffee sometimes, which came from Yemen. The money for these things came from selling cheese, perhaps some wheat, and eggs. Most women kept ten or fifteen chickens. I used to walk all the way to Hebron with just four eggs to sell, and come back with a few small things we needed – spices, embroidery silk, soap and matches from Nablus.

I think women worked harder than men. Men do the ploughing and sowing, but weeding and harvesting are women's work. One of the main things men used to do when they weren't busy with the land was going to fetch salt. They went down to the Dead Sea and bought salt in exchange for wheat or barley – and I'm sure they sometimes stole it! – and then they sold it in Hebron or Yatta. The trip took them four or five days each time; they must have spent a lot of time sitting around drinking coffee.

Building

Besides her work on her father's land (her husband was an orphan and did not have any land of his own), Umm Issa had other skills which the community needed before it had access to specialist craftsmen. Building and maintaining buildings was one communal task in which women played an important part:

> We had to work together in the old days. We didn't have money to hire people to do the work for us, and everyone knew how to do the things that needed doing, so it was natural to help each other. Plastering roofs, for instance. You might find as many as fifty people, family and close friends, working together roofing a new house or replastering an old one. It took at least four days to fetch the earth and mix it and spread it on the roof. The men's job was to mix the soil with straw and water, and spreading the plaster on the roof was women's work. It was women who plastered the walls inside the house every few years, too. My daughters used to help by carrying water and earth, but they never learned how to do the whole job. There's a great difference between my generation and the new one. Young women now may know how to make a plaster decoration on the ceiling, but that's all. People don't need the old kind of plastering so much now because there's plenty of cement and money to buy it with. Young women nowadays are only interested in embroidery, that's their main occupation!
> Another thing I used to do was building *khabi*, the mud bins we had in our houses for storing wheat and lentils and barley. They're easy to make: you bring earth from your fields and mix it with straw and water, then you build a little and leave it to dry for a few days, then you build a little bit more, and so on. The walls have to be quite high, so you can't build them all at once, the wet mud wouldn't stand up. Most people used to know how to do it. I learned from my mother. I did it for myself, and sometimes for relatives, but never for money. Now, the few young people who still use *khabi* have to pay old women to build them, they don't know how to do it themselves.

Medicine

A third and more specialised area of Umm Issa's expertise was medicine. There were various branches of traditional medicine, but no clear-cut distinctions between practitioners of one and the others. A *daya* (traditional midwife) often knew herbal medicines and massage. A *daya* was always a woman. Religious healers, in Umm Issa's experience, were always men (though this was not the case in other parts of the country). Masseurs and herbalists could be of either sex. Midwifery had more of the characteristics of a profession than other kinds of medicine; midwives often accepted payment, in money or goods, though they did not consider their practice as 'work'. Under the Jordanian administration they were accorded official status, with examinations and certification.

> My mother was famous for her medical skill, and people came to her from all the villages around Yatta and even from beyond Hebron. I learned most of what she knew and treated my own children, then after she died people started coming to me. They still do, for simple things like constipation, although there are doctors here now. I never accept payment. I say, 'My reward comes from Allah'. I used to be a *daya*, but I didn't bother to take a course and get a certificate from the government. We were away on our land a lot of the time, living in tents and caves, and nobody cared about certificates. Women had their babies out there, even in the middle of the fields sometimes. I'd deliver the baby, and we'd send its name to the *mukhtar*'s house to be registered later, when we were back in the village after the harvest was over.

Umm Issa is ambiguous in her feelings about the modern world which has pushed her own aside and scorned her skills:

> There are four or five doctors in Yatta now. They're not necessary half the time, if you ask me. A poor man works all day to get some money, and as soon as he gets home his wretched wife snatches his wallet and rushes off to take her child to the doctor, whether he feels ill or not – just to show the neighbours she can afford it. The old days were better, in my opinion. The new generation of women are lazy, they've got accustomed to an easy life. They couldn't work like I used to. They just grab their husband's money and run off to get everything they need from the shops without any trouble . . . On the other hand, we're more comfortable now. Who longs for the old days?

Control of capital

Within the circle of her densely interrelated community, Umm Issa had a valued and productive role. Many women like her had 'marketable' skills – sewing, carpet-weaving, building – which contributed to the community's welfare or the family economy, sometimes for payment, often without. Women could also accumulate capital of their own, in land, livestock, gold or cash, often by selling some of the produce of their livestock in the nearest town. The following story shows, however, that men sometimes appropriated women's property; women's notions of honour and proper behaviour could prevent them from insisting on their rights.

Umm Suleiman, only a few years younger than Umm Issa, was able to accumulate wealth for herself. Her family was richer than Umm Issa's, and her village, Beni Naim, though not far from Yatta, was (and still is) less isolated and more prosperous, with money circulating in the community earlier.

One week after my marriage (about 1945) my family gave me presents, as the custom was: one sheep and her female lamb, and one goat and her female kid. I milked them and sold the produce and soon saved enough to buy a cow and calf. After a few years I had built up the flock to thirty-five animals. It was a joke in the village that I was so lucky, my animals always had female babies, which are much more valuable than male ones.

Then my mother-in-law fell ill, and as my father-in-law had no money to pay for the doctors and medicines, he decided to sell a piece of land he had to the north of the village. We don't usually like to let land go out of the family, so my husband bought it. He had to sell my cows to do it, and the land is registered in my name. I managed to buy another cow later, and she had four calves. My husband sold them when my fourth son was born, I can't remember why, and later he sold all the sheep and goats too for a very bad price. I was never able to start my flock again because it was just at that time that my husband left us, and with eight children to feed I could never save enough money.

There was another piece of land my husband bought with my money from his brother's widow, to help her pay off a debt. When he married her, she demanded the land back so that her children would have something to inherit. My husband gave it to her, although it was my money that had bought it.

The worst thing he did, which I didn't find out about until recently, was to 'borrow' some of his sister's gold. He deposited it in a bank in Hebron in exchange for sixty dinars. He says he paid thirty dinars for a half share in a camel with a friend of his. I don't know what happened to the rest, and I never heard anything about the camel either. Then we had the 1967 war, the bank closed down, and he was never able to get his sister's gold back. Five years ago she needed the money, and to pay her back my husband had to sell our old house. We weren't living in it, but it was a big old stone one, and we were keeping animals in it.

Why didn't Umm Suleiman protest about her husband's casual disposal of her property? For the same reason that she did not take any action to demand maintenance when he deserted her to marry his brother's widow: she has a particularly rigid and self-denying notion of honour. Her belief that women's virtue lies in patience and silent endurance was always stronger than her notion of legal rights, and her conviction that she was morally superior to her husband sustained her through much suffering. If she had been firmer and insisted on managing her own property, she would probably in this case have been supported by public opinion in the village. A man who spends his wife's money is not well thought of, especially if he fritters it away or worse still spends the money of one woman on another. On the other hand, the attitude towards women's right to property is often contradictory, because of the tensions between women's legal rights, the economic needs of families as units, and women's socialisation into identifying themselves with their families. These conflicting demands still reduce women's control over their earnings in the modern economy.

Economic developments since 1967

Israel's occupation and colonisation distorted the process of economic change which had begun long before. Soon after 1967, Israeli policy-makers realised the dual economic advantages of holding on to the territories: the population of nearly a million, one quarter as big as Israel's, was a captive market for Israeli goods and a pool of cheap labour. Neglected and undeveloped by previous rulers, the economies of the West Bank and Gaza Strip were highly vulnerable to aggressive Israeli capitalism (especially as the pull of market forces was backed up by military rule). Shops were filled with Israeli goods, newly-available jobs in Israel and outside needed Palestinians' labour, and many peasant farmers became a proletariat in a high priced, relatively high-consumption international market economy. Agriculture in the occupied territories was technologically undeveloped and mostly on unirrigated hill land. It could not compete against Israeli agribusiness and became increasingly less profitable. Men left in thousands to seek waged work elsewhere, in North and South America, or in the booming oil economies of the Gulf. By 1972, 40 per cent of the workforce were commuting daily to unskilled jobs in the construction, service and manufacturing industries inside Israel.

Israel has not left it to market forces alone to shape the occupied territories' dependence on and service of the Israeli economy. Deliberate policies have hindered Palestinians from investing in their own productive base, either agricultural or industrial. Palestinian products only have access to restricted markets: they cannot be sold in Israel, where they would compete with Israeli goods. In the occupied territories they are in competition with subsidised, sometimes dumped, Israeli produce. Export channels are very limited, controlled by and subordinate to the needs of Israel in one direction, Jordan in the other. Production itself and related activities are controlled by the military government, which has the power to grant, delay or withhold permits for new buildings, changes in land use, even the replanting of fruit trees and vegetables. High taxation cuts into profits and restricts the import of plant and materials.

Two facets of occupation in particular have sparked off debate and confrontation at every level from university hall to village street: the confiscation of land and the expropriation of water. These have long-term political implications as well as immediate effects on Palestinians' lives. By the mid 1980s, over half of the land area of the occupied territories was in Israeli hands. Much of what has been taken is hill-top rather than prime agricultural land, so the direct economic effect of its loss is not always severe. Palestinians' fear and outrage are aroused by the political significance of confiscation, and by the presence in their midst of settlers committed to Israeli possession of the country and ready to use violence to achieve it.

The lack of access to water is an immediate restriction on agricultural development. The region as a whole is not rich in water. Israel, thirsty for water to sustain its industry, intensive agriculture and high standard of living, appropriates for its own use at least three-quarters of the water available in the West Bank. (Even with this inequitable distribution, shortage of water is potentially critical for the future of the state of Israel. Competition for water will be one of the more intractable problems facing the negotiators of a peace settlement in the future.)

Despite the many restrictions, overall agricultural output has

increased during the years of occupation with the introduction of
new technology in commercial market-gardens in the Jordan valley
and elsewhere. Growth has been uneven, however. The rain-fed
small farms of the hills, which used to make up over three-quarters
of agricultural land in the West Bank, have fallen into decline. The
number of Palestinians working in agriculture fell by 30 per cent
between 1970 and 1980.[1] This figure indicates an economic
transformation which has brought with it a profound restructuring
of economic and political power within villages and within families.

Nostalgia

The attitude of rural people to the changing situation of agriculture
is complex. Palestinian farmers love their land, with the
characteristic peasants' love of their own personally-owned plots
and trees and also with a more self-conscious love of agriculture in
general as it represents the Palestinian national heritage. At the
same time, farmers recognise and in some ways benefit from the
economic changes that have caused a rise in the material standard of
living as well as the decline of peasant farming. Education,
employment in the modern industrial or white-collar sector, and
higher material expectations have led younger members of rural
families to regard agricultural work with disdain, yet they still feel
an emotional attachment to their family's land.

There is a strong nostalgia for an idealised vision of the
self-sufficiency of the past and its independence from the money
economy of cities. 'We had everything we needed from our land',
'Everything is so expensive these days', 'The men have all gone
away' – these laments are heard every day. Many women feel the
land was more productive in the past, and explain this in religious
terms: 'God's grace has left us'. Their nostalgia is more than the
longing for the good old days that one finds anywhere. It is part of
the longing for the time before Israel, for the lost land and lost way
of life. Palestinians cling to an idyllic view of their past as a defence
against the dislocation, alienation and powerlessness of their lives
today.

The rosy dream of the past can exist side by side in the same
person with realistic perceptions which should logically call it into
question: that the land's lower productivity is actually caused by

neglect; that life is much easier and materially more comforable now; that the repressions and tyrannies of the past – of men over women, old over young, landlord over peasants, *hamouleh* over individuals – are collapsing as the dominance of the land over social life dwindles. Huda (see Chapter 3) revealed the power of nostalgia clearly. She despises farming and hates the repressive conservatism of village life, but as she showed me round the abandoned centre of her village with its close-packed houses, she joined a neighbour in a hymn to the past:

> Life was lovely in the past. People felt very close to one another. They lived together, ate together, worked together in the fields. Several parts of the same family all lived together, in separate rooms round a courtyard. They were never out of the sound of one another's voices. They could talk to each other all the time, and know what was happening. Our village's lands were wide and rich, full of olive and almond and walnut trees. People grew as much as the rain would produce of wheat and vegetables. They had everything they needed. Life was simple and peaceful.

Women in agriculture today

By the mid 1980s, women were performing an estimated 75 per cent of agricultural work in the occupied territories, taking a larger share as men left the land for jobs in industry. As in other countries, women's presence is proportionately much smaller in positions of power. Ownership of land, modern technical expertise and decision-making are largely in the hands of men. However, women have had to take over some tasks such as ploughing which were formerly considered 'men's work'. Many commentators, both Palestinians and outsiders, have suggested that this move into men's domain would bring women increased power and status. This does not seem to have happened. One reason is that where men are still living at home, the sexual division of power remains: it is still men who make decisions about what and where to plant. Division of labour, too, is still the norm. A landowner or one of his sons might take a few days off work to do the ploughing, or a man might be hired to do it. Most of my informants emphasised that women do occasionally plough, but this merely underlines that they do not regard it as normal.

Cultural change is another explanation for the lack of improvement in the position of women farmers. As agriculture has become the work of women, it seems to have declined in status, acquiring the stigma of 'women's work'. There are several reasons for this. First, agricultural production has declined as a proportion of the national income. Second, there has been little investment in research in and modernisation of dry hill-farming. Whether this has been the result or the cause of its low profitability, hill-farming remains technologically underdeveloped and simple – and hill-farming is the sector in which women play the most prominent role. The low profitability of farming reduces its perceived value in comparison with activities in the modern industrial and service sectors; in a money-earning economy where most families depend on wages, work on family farms which generates little cash income is marginal to the family's survival and therefore less respected.

Women as household producers

Women's farming today can be divided into three types. The first is the most widespread, where some at least of a family's men are away working and bringing or sending wages, while the women continue to work some of the family's land. They grow vegetables and fruit to supplement the family's diet, the bulk of which is purchased. They do not produce for sale and so do not generate income. Like many village women, Umm Jihad, the mother of Zeinab (Chapter 6), is objectively helping the Israeli economy by enabling her family to survive on her husband's low wage. Subjectively, she is proud of her contribution, though she would probably not acknowledge it as 'work', work being what her husband and her university-educated daughters do in places she has rarely, if ever, visited.

> My husband works in Israel and stays near his work during the week. He does most of the shopping on his way home on Fridays: meat and chickens every week, sacks of flour, rice and sugar which he brings by taxi from the next village once a month. There's still a lot for me to do – collecting firewood for the *taboun*, making bread, and growing all our vegetables. In the season there are the olives to harvest from our few trees down in the valley.

In Beni Naim, where many of the men are abroad and others work as traders, the role of agriculture is similar. Older women follow the old pattern of moving down with their flocks of sheep and goats to caves by their families' fertile valley land for several months in spring, but their daughters prefer to stay up in the village 'with their knitting machines'. Men play a small part in farming, and the village seems to have collectively concluded that farming in the old labour-intensive way is obsolete. Abu Suleiman's family, when I knew them, were very poor, because after the flush times of the 1970s the income from Suleiman's plastering business had dwindled, leaving the family, like many others, with debts and two half-built houses. However, it seems unlikely that younger members of the family will go back to farming. Suleiman's sister Munira was well-known in the village at the age of ten or eleven for her fierce energy as a goatherd, but now she is intensely conscious of what she perceives as the family's upward mobility. She is typical of many women I talked to with her mixture of romanticism and hard-headed realism. Farming has become unprofitable (for which she blames the occupation, conflating real with mythological effects – there had in fact been several years of drought at the time I interviewed her), and in her view it is hardly proper work for men any more:

We do very little farming now, and it's women who do most of it. We have a flock of sheep and goats that belongs to my father. We grow grapes on our land; that's what everyone planted a few years ago. We have to pick them, then dry them to make raisins, which we sell if there are enough. That's all the work we do except for getting the land ploughed and keeping it clear of weeds through the winter. We grow some tomatoes, to eat fresh in the season and preserve for the rest of the year. We only grow what we need for the house, nothing for sale. Men help us if they are not away at work, but we don't need them, we can do the work by ourselves.

Before Israel came, the grass used to grow tall and was enough to feed the flocks all the year round. Now it's not enough for a handful of goats. And as we don't grow much fodder, we buy what we need, though it's very expensive, and you hardly recoup the cost. Crops used to grow quickly, and the whole family was involved in taking good care of them. We grew enough wheat and barley to last us through the year. Now it's impossible, everyone says the same, everyone can tell you about land that used to be rich and is now almost barren. Land doesn't give enough to cover the cost of hiring a tractor to plough it, so people have stopped caring about it. In the past they took care of every centimetre, dug it and weeded it and repaired the walls and gave the soil a rest every few years.

Now they don't care. It is Israel which has pushed the land out of the centre of people's thoughts, by dragging them off to work there. Israel wants to drive us off our fields and make us forget about our land.

Full-time farmers

Some women farm full-time with no other major source of income. They are few in number and they are mostly women on whom the responsibility of a farm devolved when their husbands died or went abroad, abandoning them. In the past such women and their children would normally have been incorporated into the household of a male kinsman. Now their family may be so dispersed that there is no one within reach, or younger members may have adopted a nuclear-family outlook and not be eager to find space for dependent relatives.

Women alone like this are the heads of their households and are responsible for feeding their families and for making decisions in their farms. Their position does not contribute much to raising the status of women in general, because their farming is on a very small scale and largely non-commercial – a continuation, in fact, of the dying system of subsistence farming. All such women I met were elderly, and they were not expecting their daughters to follow them; their numbers must be dwindling. Like most female heads of households, they are economically marginalised and poor.

Umm Jamal stayed behind on her husband's land near Ramallah when he left to set up a shop in Brazil in 1957. Her sons followed their father to Brazil ten years later, leaving Umm Jamal with her two daughters. As long as her children were at school her husband sent her a little money from time to time, but when they grew up this stopped. He has never come home, even for a short visit, and she supposes that he has married a local woman and forgotten his previous life. 'I've never thought of going to join my husband in Brazil. What would I do there? I love my land too much, I couldn't bear to leave it.'

Umm Jamal is fairly typical of women who are full-time farmers on their own account. She works a few acres, assisted sometimes by her daughter, and does not often hire labour. She has no capital to invest, but then she does not need to expand her production, as her needs are simple. She continues to farm land which a commercial farmer would deem useless.

I grew up farming, and even when my husband was here it was I who did most of the work. He was lazy, and I managed without him. I grew figs, olives, tomatoes, grapes, wheat, everything. I had cows too. I got rid of them in 1967, because we felt so unsettled and frightened, we wanted to have as little as possible that the Israelis might take away or force us to leave. I couldn't replace them because soon after that my three sons went away and there was no one to look after them. With all the men away, my daughters and I got used to doing all the work ourselves. Did you notice the new concrete path through the garden? Butheina and I made that last summer; we carried all the stones for the foundations and mixed and poured the concrete ourselves.

Working is the only thing I love. I hate sitting still, I have to be active all day. Sometimes I start at seven in the morning and go on until eleven at night. I never know what time it is, in fact. I go out when I feel like it. If it's still dark, I sit under a tree and wait for sunrise. When people see me going down to pick my olives in the middle of the night, they say I must be a man, not a woman. But I'm not frightened, I never think about Israelis or any other dangers, I just think about the olives on the trees waiting to be picked. I want to be up there with them, like a bird in the trees.

Now I work as much of my land as I can manage by myself. The rest is just left. There are a few olive trees on it but I can't look after them; it's too expensive to hire labour, you don't get enough back to pay for it. I've never tried to rent the land out. Nobody would want it. It's stony land, not much use, and with so much lying empty, who's going to go to the trouble and expense of making mine usable? It wouldn't be worth it. It's a sad situation. The land is not happy unless you plough it and look after it all the time. It makes me cry to see it abandoned. As I picked my miserable little olive crop this year, I cried to think how my husband and sons and brothers don't care about it any more. If only my sons could come back from Brazil. But they can't, they've lost their identity cards by being away so long, and if they came back as foreigners they would have to send their children to private schools, which of course they could never afford.

It makes our Palestinian tragedy double. First we lost our country, now we're giving up the little we have left. Even the land I do farm, I don't do it properly by myself. This year I only got forty kilos of olives from my ten trees. That's nothing, hardly a harvest at all, it was just an olive here and there. But now that both my daughters are married, there's only myself to feed.

She meets her small cash needs by selling produce in the local market.

Usually I sell everything to one of the stallholders, it's easier and you get just as good a price. But if the stallholders have got as much as they need, you have to sit there and sell your produce yourself. I don't like doing that, I haven't got time to sit there all day doing nothing, just enjoying the air.

Leisure and middle-class morality

Umm Jamal is the last member of her family to farm, and when she stops working her land may well fall into disuse. The changing economic reality makes her self-sufficient, simple, hard-working life an anachronism. Young people's expectations are higher, shaped by the modern consumer economy in which they have grown up, and they are not interested in farming. The new reality and new attitudes bring ambiguous results for women. Naturally, women welcome the leisure they can have as electricity, piped water, processed foods and a few gadgets are starting to reduce the burden of their work. But money and leisure bring more questionable changes too: new standards for feminine behaviour, previously the preserve of the wealthy, come within reach of many village families. Hard-working peasant women are redefined as delicate beings who need protection, and while they are being physically liberated by new technology, their social restraints – the demands of honour – are being tightened. Munira, an enthusiastic believer in the new standards, denounced her own past as a shepherd:

> When the village families sent their daughters out with the flocks, they didn't feel it was shameful. They were ignorant and life was hard, they had to do it. But nowadays girls don't go out, their families think it is *haram* to send them. They are more aware, they know that girls can't bear the hot weather and all the walking up and down.

Umm Issa, with her longer experience and more analytical mind, has an explanation for the increased concern with sexual honour:

> This idea of shame is a modern thing. In the past we all knew one another, no strangers ever came to the village, why should we be ashamed? Women never wore a long-sleeved underdress like they do now. We just wore a *thoob* with nothing underneath. We tied the sleeves up behind our shoulders to work or carry shopping, and went around with our arms bare. There were no moral problems. Nobody looked at anyone else with the eye of sex like they do today; we were too few, and too busy. It's nowadays we have to think about shame, when boys and girls are wandering around the streets all day looking at each other.

Leisure has come because women have lost their productive role, not just in farming but in the making of domestic goods like baskets, carpets and pottery, which have been replaced by manufactured goods. Even the status-conscious Munira is beginning to perceive the futility of women's lives in the newly-wealthy village:

> There are some women who don't feel responsible for anything on their land. They're happy to live on their husband's wages. They spend all their time embroidering themselves new *thoobs*. They care too much about it, in my opinion. They have ten or even twenty *thoobs* in the house, just for variety and to show the neighbours. It is silly, when you think that each one is worth a hundred dinars [£200]. What's the point in having so many?

Perhaps some of these uselessly busy women would like to be out working and earning a salary, but in Munira's village work for women is seen as the province of the well-educated or the desperately poor, so she can only describe women's idleness in moral, not in economic, terms.

Agricultural wage-labourers

Munira's village is unusually prosperous, as is shown by the fact that only two of the old domed stone houses are still inhabited; all the rest of the families live in bright new urban-style homes. In poorer communities many women still have to work full-time, as they have in effect always done. Some of them work as wage-labourers on Israeli-owned farms in Israel or in the occupied territories; some are employed by Palestinian enterprises in the sector of agriculture which has developed most since 1967, commercial vegetable gardening. These are women whose families own no land (including refugees) or whose land is too small or for some other reason not worth farming. Umm Mohammed is a grandmother in a village in the Jordan Valley:

> Most people's land is too small to support a family. We all have to work because life has become so expensive. My husband owned thirteen and a half dunums [three and a half acres]; he died many years ago, leaving one and a half dunums to me and the rest shared between his eight sons. Water is valuable here, and when our sons started getting married and we needed to build a house, we decided to raise the money by renting out our water rights – so now we can't farm our own land. I work as a daily labourer for my neighbour Ibrahim.

Umm Mohammed's household is unusual in that two wives live together amicably in the same house, but it is fairly typical of rural areas in other respects. Besides the two older women, there are two or three daughters at home, and one married and one unmarried son. The sons work as labourers, most often in Israel, and the daughters occasionally take jobs in agriculture locally. Umm Mohammed works regularly, but her co-wife does not. All those working contribute their wages to the common family fund, which finances daily consumption as well as major expenditures such as building, marriages, education, and medical bills.

Umm Mohammed, like all other working women I talked to, feels that earning gives her 'a bit of position' and a more respected voice in family decision-making. She also values what remains of her traditional domestic production, for different reasons:

> I'm lucky that I don't have to do housework when I come home in the afternoons because my husband's other wife and my daughters do it. I rest until about four and then I take care of my little flock, eight goats and four sheep. They belong to me so I'm the one to look after them. We go out for two or three hours every evening – I like this part of the day, it's nice and peaceful – then in the milk season I milk them and make yoghurt and cheese and butter.

Women like Umm Mohammed have little power as workers and are among the worst-off as far as pay and conditions are concerned. Like agricultural labourers the world over, they belong to the poorest, least educated and most vulnerable section of society. The growth of trade unions has had little impact on them. Women's wages are even lower than men's, in agriculture and in industry. Women are not in general sole earners for their households and so they are not perceived (and do not perceive themselves) as needing a 'living wage'. Predictably the jobs women are given in the new commercial farming sector are the same relatively unskilled repetitive tasks as they did on traditional family farms – sowing, weeding and picking.

> Ibrahim employs eight or ten women, old ones like me. Most of the farmers prefer to employ women because they accept lower pay than men and they work harder; they don't keep sitting down to rest all the time. A girl is paid three shekels a day [£1.50]. I get five shekels now. That's for working from six in the morning until one or two o'clock, with

an hour's break for breakfast at ten. Do you think a man would be content with so little? No, men need about eight shekels a day. Once a big group of us, thirty-five women working on a large farm, sat down together to discuss why women are not paid the same as men. We couldn't think of any reason, except that we are women.

There are lots of women my age working. We do light jobs like weeding and picking, and younger women do heavier jobs. Generally it is men who plough and prepare the land, and lay the plastic pipes for irrigation and deal with fertilisers and sprays. We women come along and plant the seedlings after the land has been prepared, whatever the landlord tells us to plant, according to the season. Even though the jobs are light, it's quite hard work, out in the sun all day.

For women who work on Israeli farms, the conditions of work are not generally worse than in the Arab sector; sometimes, in fact, the pay is higher. Israeli commercial farms, even so-called collective *kibbutzim*, are heavily dependent on Palestinian labour:

> Agents come to the village looking for women to go and work on Israeli farms further up the valley. Lots of women go. They think they will earn more, and they do get paid six or eight shekels a day, but as far as I can see they're no better off, because they have to give half of it to the agent and pay for their transport too. The hours of work are the same, but they have to leave home at five to be there on time. I went and worked on an Israeli farm once, for twelve days. When it came to getting paid, the agent cheated me and I lost six days' wages, so I never went back again. I can't say the conditions were bad, but I prefer to work for an Arab, for someone who is like me.

For women like Umm Mohammed who are not politically active or sophisticated, political arguments against working for Israelis have no weight:

> We need the work, so we don't think about the situation much. Nobody criticises us or attacks us for working for Israelis. It's different for the agents; people do call them collaborators. They are local people. There's even a woman from our village doing it now, driving around in a car to fetch workers.

More powerful arguments against working for Israel would be concerned with honour, but Israeli use of Arab labour is so great that in many enterprises the entire workforce is Palestinian, and contact between Palestinian women workers and Israeli male bosses has been reduced to a minimum.

We hardly ever see the Israelis when we work for them. They just say hello, put us to work, and then go away. All the supervisors are Arabs. You don't feel that you are working for Israelis, you have no contact with them, so there is nothing to feel ashamed of.

Agriculture during the *intifada*

During twenty years of occupation, Palestinians in the West Bank and Gaza Strip acquiesced in dependence on the Israeli economy. Large numbers of workers abandoned the means of production they owned, their land, and moved into wage work in Israel. Small-scale farming declined to such an extent that talk of its 'death' did not seem exaggerated. In some areas larger landowners developed successful commercial farming, but saw their success undermined by decreasing profitability, the result largely of Israeli control of the market. Palestinians were bitter at the economic stagnation imposed on them but felt powerless to challenge it, and it was hard to see what form the economy of a future Palestinian state might take.

The *intifada* brought the future closer. Many factors converged to breathe a new reality and immediacy into the hitherto abstract idea of an independent state: the unexpected power of the *intifada* itself to challenge Israeli dominance, the emergence of strong local leadership, King Hussein's renunciation of Jordanian involvement in the occupied territories, and the PLO's declaration of independence. New thinking about the economy was a central component of the new mood. As leaders in the occupied territories began to draw the outlines of the future state, they focused on long-term economic planning, while for the present a campaign to disengage the occupied territories from their economic dependence on Israel and to build Palestinian self-reliance was an effective tactic for mobilising wide participation to sustain the *intifada*. Ideas which had been developing for a decade among academics and political leaders became within a couple of months powerful slogans and mass actions of defiance and hope.

The disengagement campaign can be seen as having four distinct aspects. First, withdrawing Palestinian labour and reducing consumption of Israeli goods wounded Israel economically. The second purpose was defensive: by increasing local production capacity and stocks, Palestinians could reduce their vulnerability to

Israeli reprisals. Third, revived production and marketing capacity would be the foundation for the economy of the future state. The achievements possible in these directions were limited, and perhaps the fourth function of the campaign was the most important: it united the people in an aspect of the *intifada* they all believed in and could all contribute to. It met a ready response, because economic dependence on Israel had been widely recognised and regretted, and was perceived as a weakness of the Palestinian national movement. The campaign's targets were immediate and achievable. Everyone could participate by refusing to buy Israeli goods, by supporting strikes, by suffering a loss of income without complaint, and by increasing their own domestic and local production. Women felt the effects most through their responsibility for feeding their families, and their support for the campaign was crucial.

Agriculture was central to the disengagement movement, practically and emotionally. Despite its decline as a proportion of the economy during the occupation, it is still the largest sector of the occupied territories' productive base, and it remains a potent symbol of Palestinian identity. As regards the longer-term economic future, many Palestinians see the revival of small farming as the necessary starting point. The land and the skills already exist, and low-investment, low-technology production can be expanded for processing and consumption in the local market. The disengagement campaign included calls to bring abandoned or unused land into cultivation, and the encouragement of workers to leave their jobs in Israel and return to farming. Many rural families invested in cows, goats and chickens. The image of a Palestine based on small-scale farming as in the past was politically in tune, too, with the strong democratic spirit of the *intifada*, which emphasised the power of the people and the popular base of the leadership.

Women were seen as key contributors to self-reliance. The *intifada* recognised their wider role in sustaining confrontation with the occupation, and the new economic picture placed at its centre the work that women had always been doing as small farmers and gardeners, food processors and marketers. As well as being encouraged to increase their agricultural production, women of all ages were mobilised, through neighbourhood committees and expanding networks of agricultural and women's committees, into small production groups and co-operatives to process local produce into fruit juices, jams, pickles, and baked goods.

In the rhetoric and organisation of 'self-reliance', there is evidence of the sentimentalising of women's traditional role referred to in Chapter 4. Some of the activities are exploitative and retrogressive, in effect tying women to poorly paid, low-status work; and many of the initiatives generated by the *intifada* will prove not to be economically viable. On the other hand, some of the new small enterprises are well thought-out and may survive, and many activists acknowledge that the less viable are expedient measures valuable for political reasons but not desirable in the long term. Two elements of the present activity might be of lasting benefit: the experience that will have been gained in small, co-operatively run women's enterprises, and the mood among the whole Palestinian community of recognition of and support for the important role of women in rural production.

8

Industrial work

The significant movement of women into waged work outside the home has been one of the major changes in Palestinian society since 1967: now an estimated 10–20 per cent of Palestinian wage workers are female. Several factors have combined to bring women into work. One is the increasing need for money. The material standard of living and expectations have risen exceptionally fast, boosted by the incorporation of the occupied territories into Israel's industrial and consumerist economy and by the explosion of oil wealth in the Gulf countries. At the same time the political and economic subjection of Palestinians keeps most of those in the territories poor. High prices and the low level and unreliability of men's wages push women into seeking to earn wages themselves. Second, attitudes to women working are changing as the number who actually work increases and the educational level rises. Third and most significantly, Israeli industry and agriculture, needing the cheap labour of Palestinian women, have provided job opportunities, poor though they are, that did not exist before.

For Palestinian progressives it is axiomatic that wage-work is liberating: it is the door through which women can step out of the traditional confines of the home into active participation in the public domain. Certainly at the domestic and individual level this is true, as women benefit from higher status within the family and slightly greater independence. But in a wider context, women workers can hardly be called free. The workers of the occupied territories form the lowest stratum in the Israeli economic structure, exploited by Israel's colonialism and controlled by military rule, and the position of women is lower than that of men.

Traditionally, Palestinian culture regarded it as a dishonour to a family to have women working, implying as it did that the men were incapable of providing for them and unable to keep them properly sheltered from contact with men outside the family. Apart from a few professional women (mostly teachers and nurses) only the poorest worked, and even then, in rural areas at least, it was often for local people whom they knew. When after 1948 refugees had to look for work, their justification was defiant – 'It's better to work than to go begging' – but work was still regarded as the last recourse of the desperate. Women worked only if there was no male able to support the household.

The lack of available jobs and the low status of those there were helped perpetuate this feeling, and so did the attitude of the local population towards refugees. Even within the occupied territories, where local people and refugees were of the same nation and part of the same political disaster, this seems to have been a mixture of scorn and pity, compounded by fear. Thousands of destitute refugees, amounting to 20 per cent of the existing population in the West Bank and about 75 per cent in the Gaza Strip, put pressure on land, jobs and resources, and created tensions which some refugees say they are still aware of even after twenty years of suffering together under occupation. The effect of this attitude on women's work experiences can be deduced from Nuha's memory of the early 1950s:

> Rich women used to drive into the refugee camps in their cars, dressed in their fur coats, looking for domestic servants. They would stop women in the street, look them up and down, even feel their muscles. Just like a slave market. Palestinian women were notoriously bad employers, and I'm not surprised so many refugees and rural women preferred to go and work in Israeli houses as soon as they got the chance.

Changing attitudes to work

Today, work for women is becoming more socially acceptable, though the change in attitude lags behind the facts of the situation. The degree of acceptance varies from one place to another. Where jobs are accessible, women usually take them, and their community becomes accustomed to the idea of women working. The proud claim that 'No woman in my family will ever work' is still frequently heard among the older and less educated, but as Zeinab's story showed (Chapter 6), opposition often does not survive the actual experience of women working and bringing wages home.

It is not only men whose attitude to changing customs is defiant, defensive and contradictory. Umm Mithqal, a widow in a small village in the north of the West Bank, declared roundly: 'I wouldn't send my daughter out to work, even if we were starving'. She feels that working is a sign of poverty and low social status. Her husband was a small merchant, a cut above the rest of the village, and her rejection of work can be seen as a way of asserting her social superiority, despite her present acute poverty.

> Women are supposed to stay at home and let men look after them. When a woman's husband is alive, she is alive. When he dies, she dies.

But at the same time there is an unspoken recognition that women's dependence is not absolute and immutable, but a product of particular circumstances:

> An educated woman should be able to support her family and manage everything, but we illiterate village women, who have never been responsible for anything, how can we suddenly take over when our husbands die?

Even Umm Mithqal implicitly recognises that dependence is a humiliating trap for women, and she cannot conceal her admiration for women in her own village who do work and support their families.

> How do you think a woman can manage alone if she's used to her husband doing everything for her? . . . There's a woman here whose husband died when she was thirty-two, leaving her with two children. She refused to marry again – people would have thought badly of her if she did – so she worked on her land and worked for others, ploughing and everything. I remember once she was working on the threshing floor, and the work was hard. She called to Allah, 'Allah, why did you do this to me? Why did you take my husband away when I was so young? My life is too hard.' But she managed, and brought up her children by herself. Now they all live together very comfortably.

Many older women articulate their recognition that times have changed and standards of what is respectable differ from the standards of their youth. Umm Jihad accepts that her daughters' lives will not be like her own:

> My husband earns the money. My duty is to supplement it by growing vegetables and looking after the house well. How could I earn money myself? I'm not educated. And I couldn't work in a factory and have some stranger giving me orders, I'd be ashamed. I'm not used to having strangers telling me what to do – I went straight from my father's house to my husband's. I like working on my own land, making my own bread, and being responsible for what I do. But my daughters are different. They're educated, they will always work. They haven't learned how to farm or make bread, they will always be able to buy whatever they need.

Most young women say they would like to work. More educated and demanding than previous generations, they are no longer willing to sit quietly waiting for a husband to come and claim them, but want to contribute actively to their family's welfare and earn themselves respect within the family. Some observers are sceptical about this positive desire to work, and suggest that poverty is a stronger reason, but one that people do not like to admit. A union secretary in a Jericho clothing workshop asked:

> Who would put up with such long hours and poor conditions as we do, unless she had to? Sometimes you hear a girl saying that she works because she likes it and is bored at home, but I think that if you investigated her economic situation you would find that in fact it is very bad. People don't like to broadcast the fact that they are poor.

This may be true, but nobody disputes one of the other reasons girls give for wanting to work: that it is an opportunity to get out of the house and see something of the world. In rural areas, where a woman is still not expected to leave home except for recognised and unavoidable reasons, this argument has some force. Faatmeh, who knits at home, complained:

> I would have preferred to work in a factory. It would be nice to have a change of scene and get to know different people. But my stepfather wouldn't let me. It's something about our *hamouleh* – they've got very old-fashioned ideas and they're proud of the fact that none of the girls works outside.

Zeinab says unsympathetically of her mother:

All she ever thinks about is food. If I'm sitting with her and some of my friends come in, as soon as we start talking about something outside the village, like what's happening in the university, or a strike in Ramallah, she switches off her attention and starts planning what to cook for dinner. Women who go out to work are much better, they know what you're talking about and take an intelligent interest in things outside the house.

Whether it is immediate need or the less urgent desire for greater responsibilities and broader horizons, the end result is the same. For younger women, even those who are prevented from working or who have no access to jobs, the idea of work has become familiar and normal.

Jobs available

Women's readiness to work is running ahead both of the willingness of men to allow them to and of the availability of jobs. There is not much paid agricultural work inside the occupied territories, and even if there were more, its low status means that only the poorest and most disadvantaged would accept it. The service sector, a major source of jobs for women in the West, is not so for Palestinians: women do not work in restaurants or in public transport, where they would be exposed all day long to the gaze of strangers. For the same reason they were rarely seen working in shops until recently; now they are doing so more often, in family businesses and protected from gossip by full Muslim dress. Cleaning and domestic work are available, but as elsewhere they are the lowest status of all service jobs. For educated women there is clerical and office work, and nursing and teaching, which have long been acceptable professions for women, and are still major employers.

Women with less education must seek jobs in the occupied territories' few and underdeveloped industries. There are some factories producing foodstuffs and toiletries, established before 1967, and some small pharmaceutical firms established in the early 1970s as part of a move by the PLO to create job opportunities and stem the tide of emigration. The total number of industrial jobs in the occupied territories is small, and women's unwillingness to travel into Israel for work has been turned to advantage by one sector of the Israeli economy, the clothing industry. Many

Palestinian women work in small sewing workshops doing contract work for Israeli producers. There are also Palestinian-owned workshops; conditions in these are not much better, as these shops have to compete with the Israeli industry. Women who want to work but are kept at home by domestic duties or men's authority often take in sewing or knitting for local entrepreneurs or for subcontractors to Israeli concerns (in either case, generally men). These women work hard for low pay, without enjoying the benefits that come with working in a group.

Women in industrial work

A number of mutually reinforcing factors keep women in a very weak position as workers. They suffer, as men do, the disadvantages due to the structure of the occupied territories' economy and its dependence on Israel. Palestinian industries have characteristics typical of underdevelopment, being light and low-technology. Most are small: 90 per cent of enterprises in the occupied territories employ fewer than ten people. This means that workers are isolated and heavily dependent on their employer. The weakness of the industries, high unemployment and the generally depressed economic situation all militate against the development of strength in the workforce.

Conditions and pay are poor. Labour laws exist which lay down minimum standards – forty-six working hours a week, paid religious holidays, sick leave, compensation for dismissal – but they are often flouted. Various systems of law dating from Ottoman, British, Jordanian or Egyptian and Israeli rule apply in the occupied territories, and laws relating to labour are scattered inaccessibly among them. They are not well-known either to employers or employees. One trade union organiser was uncertain whether or not equal pay legislation existed. None of the women I interviewed knew whether she was entitled to paid annual holidays, or had heard of anyone getting them; nor was anyone sure whether there was statutory maternity leave: 'None of the workers is married so it doesn't arise' was a common answer. Workers have no effective protection against infringements of the law or dismissal. In addition, some of the most exploitative features are legal. Rawda, the union organiser in Jericho already quoted, said:

Our shop is probably one of the best in the West Bank. The physical conditions are good. We have air-conditioning and a stereo system, the shop is at ground level and there is plenty of light. And we're paid a wage, not piece rate. The worst problem concerns electricity. If there is a power cut, obviously we can't work, but the boss takes the time out of our wages. In winter the electricity supply is quite erratic; it often goes off for an hour or so. We are not allowed to go home, we have to sit in the dark shop counting the minutes we're losing and waiting for the power to come back. If it is off for the whole day, we lose the whole day's wages. It's the same in all the workshops. This is the law, and the bosses meet in a committee and agree that none of them will break rank.

A significant element in Palestinian women's particular and gender-specific weakness as workers is one that women experience all over the world: they are channelled into special jobs designated as 'women's jobs', mostly classified as unskilled or semi-skilled, so they are easily replaceable and poorly paid. In one Ramallah chocolate factory, for instance, all the production is done by men, while women work as packers. Some Gaza factory owners boast that they pay women only half the wages they pay to men. The low status of the jobs and the low social status of these women reinforce each other in a vicious circle. Women's confidence as individuals is undermined by the lack of respect they receive as workers, and it is hard for them to develop the self-confidence needed to organise to make demands and raise status at work.

Every aspect of women's vulnerability as workers is exacerbated, and their ability to fight it undermined, by their social situation. Women are socialised into low self-confidence, at least in dealing with authority and the world outside the home; they are taught early to be obedient and defer to the wishes of men. Rawda:

It's easy for the bosses to treat women badly because they don't expect anything better. At the moment most women don't even think they deserve the same wages as men. Most of the girls in our shop, if you ask them anything, say, 'What do I know? I'm just a girl. What can we do? We're only women.'

The culture of honour and its obverse, shame, is thoroughly inhibiting, specifically as it relates to work, and more generally because it surrounds any self-assertion and argumentativeness with an aura of impropriety, even immorality. Thus women would expect to receive very little support from men if they tried to develop their strength. The factory worker from Jalazone camp who wouldn't tell me her name in case her fiancé in Amman heard that she was working – 'He would break off the engagement at once' – would certainly not expect him to support her if she dishonoured him by getting publicly involved in any labour dispute. Men might be happy to see their women earning money, but they do not want them to become 'unfeminine'.

Working at home

Women from traditional rural backgrounds are often the most disadvantaged as workers because they have the least social freedom. They may have received little education and be very dependent on the approval of the men of their families. Their mobility and contact with the outside world are restricted. Often they are not allowed to travel outside their village and have to do whatever work is available at home. If dressmaking or knitting on their own account are not possible, they work for contractors on whatever terms the contractors choose. Faatmeh, the niece and step-daughter of Abu Suleiman, is in this position:

My father died leaving four girls without any brothers, so I had to start working. I wanted to do it, I wanted to feel I was doing something to help. It was unusual at that time for girls to work – this was about fifteen years ago. Now it's quite common. Everyone in the family approved, though they wouldn't let me leave home to do it. I had only stayed at school until I was twelve; if I'd had more education, I'm sure I would have been allowed to go out to work. There's a big difference between people who have certificates and people who don't.

Knitting was the only work available in the village then. At one time, almost all the unmarried girls in the village were knitting. I learned to do it from my aunt, who had learned from another woman in the village. My step-father bought me a machine, and I worked for six years alone, then I taught my two younger sisters to knit, we bought another machine and worked together. After a few years' experience, I could make seven jerseys a day, working from half past seven until three. It's bitter hard work, knitting. You have to sit with the noise of the machine all day and you can never rest. A man used to come from Hebron every week to bring us the wool and collect the jerseys. The most I ever earned in a year was 200 dinars [£400], even though I only took one day off every ten days or so. I asked him for more, but he said he would make a loss if he paid us more, because he couldn't sell the jerseys for a higher price. I stopped working for him soon after that. So did everyone else, so I can't find anyone to buy my machine. Now I do embroidery, for women in the village, because people can afford to pay to have their *thoobs* made now. It's much pleasanter work, and better paid.

In practice, dependence on and obedience to the men of her family restricted Faatmeh to the most exploitative form of wage-work. As an ideal, too, the dominance of the patriarchal family has a detrimental effect on the position, and the wages, of Palestinian women. It is assumed that a woman's wages are subsidiary to the family income, which will come from a husband, brother or father. The majority of working women are in fact young and unmarried and their income goes into the collective family resources. Very few women live alone and very few, at least among poorer families, have the free disposal of their own wages. All the family's wages have to be pooled to meet major expenses such as hospital bills, further education costs, and the marriage of sons. The proportion of working women who are sole supporters of their families is small, so there is relatively little pressure of urgent need to fuel demands for better wages.

A sewing workshop

Typical household size is changing, as we have seen, in response to changing economic circumstances, and Palestinian society is moving towards a Western pattern where nuclear families are the norm. This further undermines the status of women at work: in the agricultural economy women traditionally worked in the fields, but now the role of wife-and-mother is elevated into a full-time job. Most women working in the occupied territories expect to marry, and to stop work when they do. They value themselves, as men do, as wives and mothers, not as workers, and are correspondingly less interested in improving their status at work. This is revealed by Watfa, who works in a sewing workshop in Ramallah, to which she travels eighteen kilometres every day in a shared taxi with other working women from her village:

I've worked on and off ever since I left school (at thirteen), whenever the family has needed money: in a medicine factory, in a paper tissue factory, and now sewing. At the moment my father is ill, my husband is in prison, my sister who used to work with me is pregnant, and her husband has just come out of prison and can't get a job, so I'm the only one earning for nine people. I like working, I like getting out of the house and I'm proud to practise the profession my husband encouraged me to learn, sewing. I earn 50 dinars a month [£100] out of which I have to pay 20 for transport. We work from seven-thirty until four, six days a week, with half an hour for lunch at noon. If it wasn't for the transport problem I'd be quite satisfied with my conditions. I'd like to earn more, but . . . Men do get paid more, but I think they work harder. Women are shy or ashamed or frightened to ask the boss for anything, even if they're members of the union. They're afraid of being dismissed. It would be easy for the boss to dismiss us, there are so many people looking for work. And women are not accustomed to ask for anything. I don't know how we will be able to improve our conditions . . . we have to try asking the boss first. Our boss is quite good. He's a Palestinian, he might give us our rights – though he wouldn't like it if he knew I was a union member. One problem with trying to improve the situation is that most of the girls don't really care. They are bored with their work and they hope to leave it soon. They are all unmarried except me, and very few women work after they marry. They don't have to if their husbands are working.

Working in Israel

Attitudes to work for women may vary, but there is still a general consensus that it is shameful for women to go to work in Israel. If it was, and for many still is, dishonourable to allow women to work near home and within the community, how much more so it is to let them travel far from home and work for foreigners, for enemies. There is also the fear that women will be morally corrupted by the culture of Israel. Umm Issa's condemnation is typical of the attitudes that many of the older generation express and the younger less openly subscribe to:

> It is shameful for girls to go and work in Israeli factories. They should be working in their own fields, or at least in a Palestinian factory, not with people who are strange to us and have a different religion. The only girls who go to Israel are those who don't have any men with honour to care about.

The fact that many women – around 10 per cent of the female workforce – do work in Israel, is evaded as far as possible; 'Yes, lots of women do, but not from this village, not from my family', is the usual answer to enquiries. It is acceptable for men to work in Israel but not women; this fact underlines that the objection to women going is a matter of honour, not of politics. For a few years after 1967 sections of the PLO campaigned to prevent men from acquiescing in military occupation by taking the jobs offered in Israel, but the pressure of financial need was so great and the number of men who did take jobs was so large that the campaign died down, and for nearly twenty years (until the *intifada* of 1987) men's migrating to work was only occasionally questioned. If it is acceptable for men, from a political point of view, so must it be for women. As so often in the history of so many countries, it is by the standards of sexual honour and nothing else that women are judged (and men, too, in so far as they are women's protectors).

Women who travel to work in Israel face the obstacles deriving from their social position as women, in addition to sharing with men the problems of all migrant workers. Palestinians from the occupied territories work as the lowest stratum of the Israeli economy, below Israeli Palestinians, who are themselves below Jewish Israelis. Palestinians earn on average only 60 per cent of what Israeli workers are paid for equivalent jobs. Conditions are hard, and they have little protection. The working day for migrant workers is long, as transport to work can take more than two hours. Some men, but fewer women, in fact sleep at their workplace, usually secretly as it is illegal for a Palestinian from the occupied territories to spend a night in Israel without a special permit.

More than half the workers from the occupied territories do not find their jobs through the official Israeli employment offices; in other words their work is illegal. From camps and villages they are often employed by an agent, a local person who will hire his relatives and fellow villagers and take a share (sometimes a large one) of their earnings as commission. Some women, like many men, go in the early mornings to stand in the casual labour 'markets' in and near major Israeli cities, hoping to be offered a day's work. There are advantages for both employers and employees of working outside the official system. Employers prefer it because labour hired unofficially is cheaper and lacks even the minimal protection afforded by official registration. The authorities turn a blind eye. For employees the risk of being even more open to exploitation than registered workers is often outweighed by the advantage of not having to pay union dues and taxes.

Those workers who find their jobs through Israeli employment offices in the occupied territories are officially registered and legal. They pay the same taxes as Israeli workers and are in theory entitled to some of the same benefits from the state, though seven out of ten categories of benefit are statutorily closed to them, including unemployment benefit. In practice the system is further biased against them and they rarely obtain their entitlements.

In return for payment of dues to the Histadrut, Israel's labour union, Palestinian workers get very little. The union is supposed to protect their interests, but Palestinians from the occupied territories are not allowed to become full members and cannot vote. The Histadrut is a Zionist organisation, established to protect Jewish workers. There is an obvious conflict of interests, and it is hardly surprising that the Histadrut does little for its Palestinian half-members. Nabila, a young factory worker from the Jalazone refugee camp, is typical in the low expectations she has of the Histadrut:

> I know we pay some sort of due to the Histadrut, but I don't know how much or what it is for. There is a Histadrut officer in the factory, and the Israeli workers are members. They never have to fight for their rights. They just have to snap their fingers and they get them: 'There you are and welcome!' We West Bank workers have never tried to get the Histadrut to do anything for us. I don't think we would succeed.

Nabila started working to help support a family of sixteen; her father is the only other member of the family working. She found a job in a clothing factory near Bethlehem through the Ramallah employment office. She perceives the preferential treatment of Israeli workers, but does not feel that she could do anything to change the situation:

> There are about fourteen girls from our camp working in this place. Of the two hundred workers there, more than half are from the West Bank. They're mostly girls, that's what the bosses prefer. Two cars come to the camp to pick us up at six in the morning. We are often stopped by military check-points on the road outside the camp. The boss gets angry when we arrive late at work, but when we asked him to write a letter that we could show to the soldiers so they would let us through quickly, he refused.
>
> We work from seven until four-thirty five days a week, with twenty-five minutes break for breakfast and half an hour for lunch. The employer pays for our meals and for our transport. We usually get home around six. The Israeli workers have better conditions. They work from

eight until three-thirty for the same basic pay, and if one of them wants to leave early she can easily get permission. If one of us wanted to leave early, she'd have a hundred fights before they'd let her.

Sometimes we are told we must work late, or on Fridays – told, not asked, and we don't get extra pay. We know this is illegal, we should get time-and-a-half for working overtime. But nobody ever refuses. For one thing, on weekdays it would be impossible for us to get home until the boss sends the cars for us. Most of the girls have not been working in the factory long, and they are afraid of being dismissed if they refuse. If anyone who has worked there longer tries to complain – some of them have been there as much as eight years – the boss just offers them a little extra money and they shut up.

The Israeli workers are paid more than us. They get about 300 shekels a month [under £150], while we usually have about 200 to take home. We work on a quota system. You get a fixed rate for fulfilling a certain quota, as long as it is up to standard; if you do more, you get paid extra, but not at the full rate. It's hard to understand how much you are supposed to be paid. After I'd done my training month on half-pay and started on full pay, I was getting less than the other workers for the first couple of months. I didn't understand why, and was afraid to ask. The pay-slips are big computer-printed sheets with all the totals and deductions listed in Hebrew. It's hard to check that you are getting what you should be.

Palestinian trade unions

Nabila sounds fatalistic and even uninterested in the possibility of improving her situation at work, but she has in fact taken the positive step of joining the local branch of the Sewing Workers' Union. Though the Palestinian unions, based in the occupied territories, are not recognised in Israel, they are trying to build up their membership among workers there. They do not have much strength to organise collective action, but they can play an educational role and help workers individually. One task is to help workers understand their pay-slips and know their entitlements. Another is to help employees bring cases against employers who default on their duties. Unions can give advice and seek assistance for their members from a growing network of lawyers, both Palestinian and Israeli, who are interested in such cases. So far, however, as a local organiser ruefully admitted, the trade unions 'haven't made much headway among sewing workers. These are mostly young women, waiting to get married, and they don't see the importance of union membership'.

Without a government of their own which might devise and implement a labour policy in their interests, Palestinian workers are at the mercy of the forces of Israeli colonialism and the occupied territories' own industrial capitalism developing under Israel's shadow. The trade union movement is beginning to emerge in the face of considerable difficulties. Palestinian society has no tradition of horizontal class-based solidarity. The economy is not highly industrialised, three-quarters of the population live in rural areas, and the organisation of much work – in small units, in service industries, or as casual migrant labour – makes it difficult to reach many workers. High unemployment or underemployment and the poor economic environment discourage union membership, and the unions have insufficient financial resources. Nonetheless they form a significant part of the emerging Palestinian national entity. Their importance is increased by the political significance that any indigenous organisation developing under occupation is bound to have.

There have been trade unions in Palestine since the 1920s, but the recent history of the movement begins in 1963, when the Palestine Trade Union Federation was established in the Jordanian-ruled West Bank. At the beginning of the occupation, because of the high level of political and military resistance in the Gaza Strip, the military authorities refused to grant a permit to the Gaza Trade Union Federation, which was only allowed to resume its activities in 1979. In the West Bank the trade unions have been gaining steadily in confidence and recognition. The military government has granted very few new licences since 1967, but new unions have been set up which have to operate semi-legally, sharing the licences of previously existing unions.

Palestinian trade unions are local groups rather than nation-wide institutions. Some are trade-specific, but many are general. Today many small unions are linked at national level in general federations for the West Bank and Gaza Strip. Together they have gained the adherence of an estimated 30 per cent of the male workforce, and 10 per cent of the female. Besides successful strikes and negotiations for improved pay and conditions, they offer advice and social, welfare and educational services to their members.

The growth of trade unionism is hindered more by the political situation under occupation than by social and economic conditions. Conflict with the occupation authorities is intrinsic in the unions' very existence: as self-governing Palestinian institutions they constitute a threat to the military government's control. Consequently, although in principle trade unions are allowed to function, in practice they face many restrictions. They are kept under constant surveillance and activities such as recruitment, meetings and elections are regularly obstructed. Military forces routinely raid union offices, confiscate union publications and records (especially membership lists), harass and arrest activists and officers, and threaten and intimidate rank-and-file members. The atmosphere of fear this creates is as damaging to unions' growth as the repressive acts themselves. Amal Wihdan, a leading unionist (who at the time of writing was under house arrest because of her union activities) comments:

> The authorities are clever: by raiding union offices and confiscating papers and so on, they make ordinary people equate union membership with personal danger, and people think twice before setting foot inside a union's office.

Fear also makes employers more hostile to unions than simple commercial interest would; they see unions as bringing trouble from the military authorities.

To justify their actions the Israeli authorities charge that the trade union movement is an arm of the PLO (which is banned in the occupied territories) and that trade unions spend more time in political activity than in organising labour. To some extent these are self-fulfilling prophecies. Regular attacks raise the political temperature and force the unions into the position of fighting against the authorities for their survival. Defence of the workers' right to organise becomes defiance of the occupation. Besides, the unions have limited resources to carry on their work of organising labour, as Amal points out:

> The unions put the maximum effort possible into their work, but how much can they do when half their active members are in prison and the other half under town arrest?

One does not have to see the hand of the PLO directing the trade unions, as the Israeli government does, in order to understand the role unions play in national political life. Being among the few national institutions existing in the occupied territories, they naturally become channels for the expression of political will and common national identity. They reflect people's commitment to the PLO and support for different groups within it. There are so few elections of any kind under military occupation that elections to trade union committees tend to serve as political platforms. Political needs cannot be ignored, but Palestinians are aware of the danger that they might divert energy from the struggle for labour rights, and at times the union movement has been weakened by interfactional rivalry and splits.

When employers and employees are united in their sufferings under occupation and in their commitment to national struggle, how far can workers go in fighting for their own particular rights or class interests? Amal feels that although this is a problem in the short term, it is one that can be solved with patience and good judgement:

> Palestinian workers are as aware as anyone else of their class position in society. The national unity between workers and bosses does not obscure the class contradiciton between them. The union I belong to tries not to let the class contradiction come to the surface. When we have a problem of workers' rights to deal with, if we feel that the owner has an important role in the national economy, we try to solve the problem through negotiation in order to damage the industry as little as possible. We only use strikes as a last resort. We do not feel that this weakens our struggle as unions. A solution that harmed the national economy would harm the national cause, which is also our cause. Employers do try to exploit our national feelings, it is true. They say, 'It is your duty to keep on working. If you strike you are traitors', and so on. We never accept a solution based on national considerations at the expense of the working class. We always insist that workers' rights are basic and not negotiable. But we are not ready to fly the flag of all-out class war yet. We must delay it until we have our national freedom. If we started to wage it now, it would lead to Palestinians fighting against Palestinians, and where would that get us?

Challenges for women trade unionists

Women have their own particular difficulties in organising themselves as workers, deriving from their social position. Amal again:

> Women's participation in the workforce has grown since 1967, but their involvement in unions has not grown proportionately. The majority of

working women have become elements of production without achieving participation in the union movement.

Some of the difficulties are familiar to women everywhere. Women are accustomed to giving home and family the first share of their time and attention, so the first hurdle is to win their commitment to participation in unions. Even when commitment is achieved, time is a problem. Transport from rural areas to workplace adds considerably to the length of the working day. Most women are under strong pressure to give all available time to family and social duties, and household work is time-consuming. As one working woman in Jericho put it, 'Women won't be liberated here until men stop demanding stuffed vine leaves for their dinner!' Even politically active women are often not confident enough of their belief in equality to demand that men share in household tasks, and few men are prepared to do so.

Other difficulties arise from the honour system and the 'protection' of women. A woman's family will not accept her going to meetings with men or being out of the house in the evening. They are not willing to let her risk getting into trouble with the military authorities: this is feared not just for itself but for the dishonour it brings on the woman and her family. The woman herself cannot afford to get a bad reputation. Amal believes,

The increase in numbers of women unionists is itself an important step in overcoming these social barriers. A woman can go to a meeting if there are ten other women there, but not if she is the only female. We had an example of this recently. There were two active women on the administrative board of the Sewing Workers' Union in the Tulkarm area. The military government began to summon the board members one by one for questioning. One of these women was forced by her family to withdraw from the board. Then the other, being the only female there, had to drop out too. It is clear that the only way to deal with society's fears is to enrol large numbers of women in unions, and then some of these problems will solve themselves.

The unions themselves have not been positive enough, in Amal's view, in approaching the problems of women:

The unions do not have free access to women, because the activists are mainly men. And until recently they were not paying much attention to women members and their specific problems. It wasn't really hostility, just indifference, partly because of the continuance of traditional male thinking, partly because with all the difficulties and harassments unions face, women's situation was not a priority. They had no programme planned to help women become involved.

With all the constraints unions work under, what can they offer women, and what steps are being taken to increase women's representation and participation? The most frequently heard answers are linked: education and consciousness-raising, for women as unequal members of society and as workers. In Rawda's view, 'improving women's self-image is one of the principal tasks'. Amal, who in addition to her union position is also a member of the Executive Committee of the Palestinian Federation of Women's Action Committees (see Chapter 10), explains how the committees can help build women's confidence and participation:

> The Women's Action Committees have set it as one of their prime tasks to be a bridge to help women join unions. We do not set ourselves up as an alternative to trade unions, because we feel it is necessary for women to belong to the same representative bodies as men; but we believe women need special sections in the unions, because of the social prohibitions on their sharing in the same organisations with men, and in order to deal more sensitively with their special problems. We try to bring women first into our committees as members, and there we hold lectures about women's role in society, their rights, their unions and the unions' role as workers' representatives. Step by step we can prepare them for full participation in their respective unions.
>
> We help women see how much their oppression as workers results from their oppression as women. They know that women in factories have a lower position than men. For instance, why are women usually dismissed from their jobs when they get married? Factory owners do not want married women workers who might have other priorities in their lives than work, and they don't want to be troubled with giving them maternity leave and special consideration because of their children. There is no law, or at least no effective law, preventing them from firing women who marry – according to the Jordanian labour law, which is very reactionary, an employer can usually get away with paying compensation. I can't think of a single case of a union winning someone's reinstatement into her job, but unions can give moral and practical support, helping dismissed workers to get their full compensation. This is particularly important for workers in Israel, where the employers often try to get away without paying, because they think all Palestinian workers are defenceless and ignorant. All women should at least know what their legal rights are at work.
>
> Women's level of ordinary membership of unions is still very low, but at higher levels women are over-represented in proportion to their membership base. This must say something about their leadership qualities, mustn't it?

9

Politics and the national struggle

From their need to justify their own nationhood by denying that of Palestinians, Zionists volunteer Jordan as an equally valid home for Palestinians and point out that the concept of a Palestinian 'nation' is of recent origin. This is true, but it is irrelevant. Nation states are one of the basic political facts of twentieth-century life, and the Palestinian nation is not the only one to have been brought into the world by colonialism. To ask whether a particular nation state is right or wrong, does or does not have 'the right to exist', is a false question, ignoring the historical fact of the complex and expedient development of any nation. For at least twenty years Palestinians have identified themselves as a nation, and as such they demand the rights accepted in the twentieth century as belonging to nations. They also have rights as individuals, and these are violated by the Zionist claim to exclusive possession of the land of Palestine. Displacing or desiring to displace an entire population and expecting them all to emigrate and leave their beloved land ignores humanity and cannot easily be argued away.

From their restricted position in society, Palestinian women have not been able to take part as publicly as men in the national movement. They lent their support to fighters but were excluded from decision-making and responsibility, which were the province at local level of *hamouleh* patriarchs and village councils consisting of the patriarchs, and at the national level of the members of the large wealthy families. However, some women were active: a few rural women took up arms in 1936 and 1948, and groups of urban women mobilised their power into moral appeals. From these isolated beginnings the participation of women has grown, and now women contribute fighters, voters, candidates and acknowledged

135

leaders to the national cause. Their numbers are still not large, but they are more than tokens; they are a real presence in the national struggle.

The sense of loss

All Palestinians live with the consciousness of loss – loss of their land and loss of what the land represented for the community. Those who were expelled or who witnessed defeat, remember. Those born since 1948 have lived the loss in imagination through their elders' oft-repeated stories and the sad recurring images of post-1948 Palestinian poetry and art.

Zuhur, a teacher in Hebron, is typical of many in the passion and also the ambiguity of her attachment to the lost land. Born in 1950 of a refugee family, she grew up hearing her father mourning his farm, which in retrospect has acquired the perfection of an earthly paradise: 'I used to have one hundred dunums of land as flat as your palm and so fertile you could harvest from it four times a year. Now I haven't even got enough land to dig my grave.' Zuhur is surrounded by her parents' pain. She told me:

> They are always talking about the disaster and the change in their lives. They remember their happiness in the past, when they used to sit with all the twenty-five members of the family around them, singing and telling stories. Those twenty-five have never been together again since 1948. Now my brothers are scattered all over the world, not even allowed to return to visit their father on his deathbed.

For the predominantly peasant Palestinians, land was not just their material home and livelihood, but also the basis of social organisation and self-valuation. Land is homeland, the foundation without which a community and its members feel incomplete. The bitterness of her life as a refugee has taught Zuhur to feel this passionately:

> Without your homeland, you can lead an existence, earn money, but an essential part of you is missing.

When it comes to the political meaning of 'homeland', Zuhur is torn. Supposing Israel withdrew from the occupied territories and allowed Palestinians to establish a state on these truncated fragments of their historic land. That would be the restoration of some of Palestinians' political rights and would form the basis for their recognition as a nation, but Zuhur's emotional attachment to her own ancestral lands is stronger than political principle. Like all refugees, she knows that the village her parents remember was deliberately destroyed after 1948, that their fields have been obliterated under modern suburbs or industrial agriculture, and that the Israelis living there are not likely to leave. She knows her loss is irreparable. That does not make it any less painful or less unjust.

Individuals' political awakening

If the spirit of resistance is born of loss and denial of political rights, it is reinforced every day for Palestinians in the occupied territories by the humiliations and injustices of life under military rule. For everyone in the West Bank and Gaza Strip, the force of the occupation intrudes into all aspects of daily life. Women are direct victims less often than men, but interference and violence are all around them. For many political activists it has been the constant sight of the occupation, rather than any particular incident, that has awakened their sense of national duty. Salwa (see Chapter 5), who was imprisoned at the age of sixteen:

> When you are a child, everything you see affects you. You see soldiers pushing their way into houses. You go into other houses yourself and see everyone crying and when you ask why, they say 'They took our son', 'They took our father'. At night you hear an explosion: 'What's that?' 'They're blowing up a house'. You see soldiers spraying tear-gas and shooting at demonstrations in the street. You are a small child, and at first you are frightened. But when I was a little older, being a *feda'i* was all we dreamed of, me and my friends. Whenever you saw children playing, and asked them 'What are you doing?', the answer was 'I'm a *feda'i*, and she's my enemy'.

Amneh, a teacher of the deaf:

> I was in Jordan in 1970, during 'Black September' when the PLO was being driven out of Jordan. It was agony to see how everyone was

fighting against our people and trying to drive them away, again and again. Meanwhile at home in the West Bank I was seeing strangers in our land, seeing how they were able to put checkposts on roads and stop and search us four or five times a day. Even in our own country we weren't free.

Individual defiance

These two women, young and educated, had the opportunity to join an organised movement. Most women do not, being confined to their homes and isolated from the outside world by social convention, lack of education, and household responsibilities. But the pressure of the occupation on them is as great: 'We walk in fire – how can we not feel it?', one older woman in a literacy class said to me. They may not be leaders or political theorists, but women are individuals with homes and families, and as individuals they react strongly when their families' safety, freedom and property are attacked. With whatever means they have they oppose the brutalities of the occupation. Often women seem to be more courageous and defiant than men. This may be partly because they are less likely than men to be victims of violence or imprisonment, but a Ramallah academic, commenting on the acclaimed role of women in the *intifada*, suggested another explanation:

> You often hear it said that Palestinian women are stronger than men. It's remarkable how when it comes to confronting the army and confronting their own fear, it's women who do it first. I think it's because women have been oppressed for so long – wherever they are, they have had to fight to get there. In their families girls have to fight for any freedoms, whereas boys have everything handed to them as a right. Women have had an accumulation of experience of oppression, so there's an explosion of reaction.

Individual women's defiance is celebrated in the constant retelling to families, neighbours and visitors of heroic anecdotes. I met a grandmother who had stood hurling her shoes at the driver of a bulldozer as it advanced to uproot her olive trees. A mother who had tried to push her way into prison to visit her son on a day when visits were forbidden declared proudly, 'The guards knocked my teeth out!' Umm Ibrahim, a refugee mother of seven whose husband, the breadwinner, had been arrested, walked miles through snow to challenge the local military governor:

> You've got three choices. You can shoot us all, and our troubles will be over; or you can imprison us all, and at least we'll be fed; or you can release my husband, so that he can support us.

The culture of the national movement

Women like these may be separated from each other as regards action by their social situation, but psychologically they are not isolated from the shared struggle. The Palestinian national movement has created a language of shared images and concepts, a rhetoric of heroic resistance, a body of inspirational stories. Shared by the least educated as well as the elite, this rhetorical unity contributes to the high morale the people maintain despite their years of suffering and the stress of life under occupation. It is epitomised by the prisoner's mother who said, 'All prisoners are my sons. I fear for them all, and I am proud of them all.'

One important element of this unity is the shared understanding of their situation, a common currency even among the least educated. Understanding events, instead of being merely their victim, helps produce the self-respect and courage that persist in the face of setbacks. Palestinians have discovered this, and the level of political and historical consciousness is strikingly high. Ask even a village woman with no schooling who has spent her life working on her husband's land, and she is likely to explain her present state in a wide context of history, Arab politics and superpower rivalry. Seventy-six-year-old Naima in Deheisheh refugee camp was not unusual. Telling me the story of her life, she commented:

> When the English came in 1918, we in our village had never heard of them. It was as if they just appeared out of the Jaffa Sea. At that time they controlled the whole Arab world, except the French bits. We welcomed them at first, they did a lot of good for us. But they were just fattening us up for the Zionists, like lambs for the slaughter.

The feeling of unity is built up by the constant reiteration of anecdotes, of history, and of the pictorial symbols that have become icons of the national liberation movement – the black and white checked *kefiyye*, portraits of the most famous of those who have died, pictures built up from a pool of simple symbolic images of chains, roots, olive trees, doves, and maps of Palestine.

'Sumud' – steadfastness

A helpless population, waiting for a solution from outside, could easily have slid into apathy, despair and disunity; but the tactic of *sumud* could unite the occupied people and imbue their least significant action with meaning. *Sumud* integrated women into the national movement as easily as men, as it demands exactly the virtues contained in the traditional ideal of women's character – patient endurance, silent strength, self-sacrifice, duty.

There is *sumud*, for example, in the attitude of refugees to their physically miserable life in camps. They do not want to move away and build better houses elsewhere, because this could be interpreted as accepting their expulsion as permanent, dissolving the refugee presence which constitutes the concrete proof of Israel's injustice, and forfeiting their claim to reparation. Umm Ibrahim, who has lived for nearly forty years in the same two-room house built by UNRWA in a camp near Hebron, does not feel she has a choice:

> As long as we live here we are still Palestinians. It is better to stay here, exposed to the rain and the sun, than to live in comfort but to lose our identity as Palestinians.

Mrs Yusef, a member of one of Ramallah's prominent bourgeois families, was describing *sumud* as she told me how the tactics of resistance have changed since 1967:

> At first, after the occupation began, we thought we could bring it quickly to an end. We appealed to international opinion with big, organised demonstrations. We don't hold such demonstrations much any more. Not because we've accepted the occupation or have given up in despair, but the opposite: as we've realised that the occupation is long-term, and we can't expect support from anywhere else, and as Israeli repression has increased, we've realised that different tactics are called for. It was when the Israeli authorities started deporting people in large numbers that one began to think, 'Is a demonstration worth the risk of being deported? No, the most important thing is to stay here, above all else.'

Using the feminine role

Many women have acted in defence of the individual rights of their families; many more have had the opportunity to contribute on a wider scale, protecting groups and movements. In either case, for the vast majority of women until recently, their actions have been responses to circumstances, reactions to what other people do around them. The scope of their actions has mostly been confined within women's conventional social role. Their involvement might be the result of personal understanding and commitment, and the tasks they undertake might be fraught with danger, but women have mostly been limited to supporting men's initiatives rather than initiating or leading actions themselves. They could not directly influence events or have any political impact. Political and cultural leaders have been happy to celebrate women's participation in this subordinate way, as we have already seen.

Some women, not surprisingly, have been frustrated by the passivity of the role allotted to them. Umm Fawwaz, for example, risked her freedom to help her brother's communist group – whose aims and ideals she shared – during the repressive Jordanian era, hiding the group's typewriter in her house.

> I lived in a flat over the police station, but nobody would ever have thought of looking for a cache of anything in the house of a woman living by herself with a baby – not Jordanian soldiers, anyway, who were notorious for their stupidity!

But she sensed in herself greater potential for action than society allowed her to develop, and ended her story with a wry joke: 'If I knew how to read and write, I would have changed the world!' (Umm Fawwaz is one of several older women I met – Umm Ibrahim is another – who have been conscious throughout their lives of being excluded from political power because of their social class as well as gender. These women's attitudes to politics and leadership is generally one of alienation, scorn and distrust. I have not had the opportunity to find out whether the *intifada* has overcome their scepticism.)

Women can become politically effective when they cross the boundary from individual into collective action. To do this, they have to challenge their gender-imposed isolation and lack of confidence, but do not otherwise have to abandon their 'feminine' roles. On the contrary, the majority of women's actions even during the *intifada* have made use of, rather than overridden, the protection traditionally owed by men to femininity. Women's presumed 'innocence' and their status as the repositories of men's honour are acknowledged, even between enemies, and their supposed weakness and their sacredness as mothers have moral force and practical uses which women in struggles all over the world have recognised and utilised. Mrs Yusef, who was herself active in demonstrations of protest against the occupation in 1967, recalls:

> In the early days after the occupation began, it was our women who led the way in resistance. Some of our activities were carefully planned. We thought that if we Palestinians called the world's attention to our injuries in the most moral and peaceful way possible, the world would understand and couldn't fail to help us. We concentrated our efforts on the Holy Places in Jerusalem. For instance, twelve women held a three-day sit-in in the Church of the Holy Sepulchre. Of course, it turned out that our hopes were naive. We know now that moral appeals have no effect. We've seen the massacres of Sabra and Shatila come and go without bringing any practical changes.
>
> Some of our demonstrations, on the other hand, arose spontaneously. It was traditional for women to visit the graves of martyrs, and the big processions we made, all dressed in black, to the graves of fighters killed in 1948 and 1967, grew into powerful demonstrations of national feeling. Israeli troops stood by, and didn't like to shoot us because we were women. This is why we could do things that men couldn't. When men, especially students, tried to mount any protests, they were the targets of violent and fierce repression. This put them off at first until they became bolder and more audacious after 1974. That was the year Arafat spoke before the United Nations, and we all became more confident.

Popular demonstrations

Women have played a crucial role in the spontaneous mass demonstrations that have been a significant feature of the *intifada*. They had done so before, as the following account shows. The occasion of this demonstration in spring 1982 was the Israeli government's decision to replace its military rule of the West Bank with so-called 'civilian administration'. The move was to make no substantial difference to life for Palestinians, but was merely designed to whitewash the fact of continuing military rule. The

Palestinian people rejected the plan, and their elected town leaders refused to accord the new administration legitimacy by co-operating with it. Yusra, a thirty-three-year-old housewife and grandmother who took enthusiastic part in the protest demonstration in El Bireh, near Ramallah, was in no doubt about who initiated the policy of non-co-operation:

The El Bireh Day, they call it. It was the people of El Bireh who made it into a triumph; our mayor would never have done it by himself. We were surprised when he shut the door in the face of the civilian administration officer. I'm from the same family as him, and I know that all the men of the family are cowards!

It was about eight o'clock in the morning. Word soon spread all over the town that soldiers were trying to take over the town hall. People started gathering in front of it, then a young man went into the mosque and called out over the loudspeaker, 'Girls of El Bireh, brave women, come to your town hall, the soldiers are invading it!' So we all went, everyone in the town, but especially women, hundreds and hundreds of them. We threw stones at the soldiers as we passed them, grabbed them and hit them. You can't imagine what a sea of people there was outside the town hall, all shouting 'The people of Palestine!' and *'Feda'iin! Feda'iin!'* There were soldiers all around the town hall. They threw tear-gas canisters into the crowd, and then started shooting over our heads. Then they shot one young man straight through the heart . . .

Half the crowd followed the boy to the hospital and stood outside to see what happened to him. He died almost at once. Soldiers were posted all round the hospital and tried to disperse us but we wouldn't go away; we knew that the army would try to take the body away and hide it so that they could pretend the death never happened. Some of our young men smuggled the body out through the kitchen door, without the soldiers seeing, and carried it away on their shoulders towards the graveyard.

What a funeral procession he had! The dead boy was in the middle, men carrying him and surrounding him, then all the women and children around the outside of the procession, to stop the soldiers attacking the men and snatching away the body. There were so many of us, they couldn't stop us. We reached the graveyard safely and buried him.

All the way home, the soldiers were following us, hitting us. We were so wild that day, especially the women, because of seeing one of our boys killed in cold blood, that we were hardly aware of what we were doing. I was so furious, I had no fear at all. I was thinking, 'You only die once, who cares if it's today'. I saw a group of soldiers standing round a taxi full of children; they had taken the driver's identity card so he couldn't drive on, and the children had been there for hours, weeping with terror. I grabbed one of the soldiers by the shirt and shouted at him, 'Throw your gun down, and then we'll see who's the strongest, you or me!' 'I'm only following orders', he said. 'Well, I can see you haven't got any brothers and sisters', I said and really I shamed him into giving back the driver's identity card – he hurled it on to the ground in front of him.

All the way home I was convinced I was going to be shot. I was saying 'Allah have mercy on me', with every step. If I was going to die, I must at least die a good Muslim death. When I reached home it was five o'clock. I had been out since eight, and I hadn't given a thought to my children all day, I had forgotten they existed.

From spontaneous to organised resistance

Demonstrations like these can sometimes make certain short-term gains, obstructing some of the occupiers' intentions, maintaining the refusal to grant the occupation legitimacy. They certainly form scenes in the important mythology of resistance: this one, until it was superseded by the more dramatic events of the 1987–8 *intifada*, was an often mentioned, often re-lived reference point. But it is difficult to develop this kind of spontaneous demonstration as a method of resistance, and the difficulties are in part related to the fact that a large proportion of their participants are women. The majority of women are not members of any organisations, political or otherwise, so their potential cannot be directed. They are tied by domestic duties and fears, and unaccustomed to acting on their own account. The events that bring them out on to the streets tend to be local, their protests defensive, rather than national, offensive, and initiative-seeking. This was still true in the first months of the *intifada*, when widespread outbreaks of protest were constantly refuelled by the mounting toll of deaths and brutality.

Throughout the period of the occupation and previously in the 1948–67 period, there have been some attempts at organised non-violent protest, using women and the feminine role to appeal to institutional and public opinion. Women refugees held sit-down demonstrations in refugee camps in the 1950s, demanding fairer distributions and services from UNRWA. The mothers of prisoners have regularly staged sit-ins around the offices of the Red Cross, appealing for more energetic intervention to protect the rights of prisoners. Some of these demonstrations have been admirable feats of endurance, but they have come to seem rather more ritualistic than hopeful, and the participants have appeared afraid of risking more exposed and public protests.

A sustained programme of civil disobedience, which women would be well placed to carry out, had never been tried before the *intifada*. There was a widely held feeling that non-violent resistance is futile, for the lesson of life under occupation is that the Israeli army have no scruples about using force to crush it. Palestinians have generally felt that the solution to their problem would come from military or diplomatic activities outside the occupied territories. Perhaps the *intifada* will have made a lasting change to this view: one of the reasons for its strength has been that its leaders have grappled with the problem of how to change gear and transform spontaneous local reaction into sustained mass action.

Armed struggle: women in support roles

Among the traditionally feminine roles in national struggle, the one with the longest history is that of supporting fighters. In the early battles of Islam, women had an honourable place beside the battlefield cheering men on and giving them first aid. In recent history, too, women have helped guerrilla fighters by hiding them and carrying arms, food and first aid. Naima in Deheisheh camp recalls one incident, more memorable than many other similar ones, from the 1936 revolt against the British mandate:

> I lived at the end of our village, so the *feda'iin* who were hiding in the mountains used to come secretly to my house and I gave them bread and butter and eggs from my hens, and sometimes cooked meals for them. One came to me when he'd been hit by ten bullets. I hid him in my cowshed and brought a doctor from the next town to treat him. One day British troops surrounded the village, sealed off all the exits, and started to search for him. I tried to think how I could save him. In an olive grove near my house there was a big old olive tree, what we called a Roman tree. It was so old the trunk was hollow and open at the top. I took some cushions and a jar of water and put them in the trunk, then the guerrilla climbed in after them. I went back to my house, and minutes later the soldiers were round gathering us all together in the centre of the village while they made their search. I was terrified they would find my *feda'i*, for if they did, they would hang him.
>
> When they'd released us and left, I went running out to the tree to see if he was safe. As I came near, I saw that the ground under the tree was littered with empty corned-beef cans.
>
> 'Are you alright?' I asked. 'What happened?'
>
> 'They chose this tree to have their lunch under! They were all here, opening their tins of meat, laughing and joking. I could hear every word they said!'
>
> 'And you managed not to cough or sneeze!'

Gaza in the early days of occupation

Naima, as a married woman, had some freedom of movement. For young girls family pressure was, and still is, far more likely to keep them safely at home, away from the risk of dishonourable contact with the enemy. Layla, the following speaker, was fortunate in having a family who supported her wish to join in the struggle. She lives in Jabalya refugee camp in the Gaza Strip, where for a few years after 1967 armed resistance was strong enough to present a serious challenge to the Israeli occupation. She was fifteen when she joined an underground first-aid unit. Her account shows that supporting fighters is by no means an easy option.

My job was to help *feda'iin* who were wounded in the course of their actions against army patrols. The army would cordon off the area where an action had taken place. I would have to slip through the cordon, making sure I wasn't seen, find the wounded fighter, give him first aid, take his weapons in case he was caught, and make my way back unseen through the cordon.

One day a message reached me that two *feda'iin*, Ayoub the leader of my group and another called Ibrahim, had been wounded and were hiding in a village nearby. Helicopters were already surveying the area. I found a nurse, and carrying first-aid equipment we tried to get into the village. We were turned back as a curfew had been imposed. The second time we tried, we put on long village dresses and pretended we lived there . . . We went to the place we had been told the *feda'iin* were lying, but there was nothing there except blood on the ground, still wet, and soldiers everywhere searching for them. The nurse was frightened and went back to the village and I went on searching by myself.

I can still remember what happened next as clearly as if I am seeing it in a film. I found Ayoub, and went back to fetch the nurse. As we returned together, he saw us, turned his head to show us where to look for Ibrahim, and died.

We were at one end of an orange grove. There were soldiers searching at the other end, so we couldn't risk carrying Ayoub's weapons away with us. As we crossed into the next orchard, a soldier stopped us. 'Where are you going?' 'Into our orchard to pick some fruit.' 'Go home, there is a curfew, no one is allowed to come into the orchards at the moment.' My companion did as she was told, but I managed to slip past the checkpoint by myself.

I walked along, and after a while I heard breathing close by. I looked over a wall, and found Ibrahim, lying under a tree, injured in both legs. There were soldiers only twenty or thirty metres away, we could see their legs through the trees. But orange groves are very dense, and when I had fetched the nurse from the village we were able to help Ibrahim limp

away, without making a sound, and the soldiers didn't see us. We got him
into a car beyond the cordon, and away to safety.

Joining the armed struggle

Layla found that it was a small step from dangerous and difficult
work like this to military action:

> The fighters in the company had seen how good I was. They accepted me
> as a comrade and treated me as an equal, although I was only the second
> girl from Gaza to become active as a soldier. I had to be prepared to act in
> the same way and suffer as much as any of the men in the group. In fact I
> could often do more than they could, because whenever a man moved
> around the streets he was likely to be followed, whereas a girl could walk
> about without anyone paying any attention to her.

The number of women who have joined military cells of the
resistance movement in the occupied territories has been small,
though significant. For all those I talked with, as for Layla, the
decision to take up arms was a natural development from childhood
experiences of life under military occupation. This is how Layla
began the story of her life:

> From the age of six or seven I was always hearing about Palestine, about
> my village and its fields and orange groves, and how the Israelis came and
> we lost it all. I dreamed of joining the army and fighting to get everything
> back.

The Israeli invasion of 1967 took most Palestinians by surprise, and
Layla was playing in the alleys of the camp as the bombs began to
fall.

> Whenever I heard the sound of a bomb, or screaming, I ran to look, I
> didn't know any better. The worst thing I saw was a neighbour of ours,
> who had been nursing her baby. A bomb had blown her leg off. She died,
> and the baby just went on sucking.

Scenes like these are fixed in Layla's mind – evidence, she feels, that
the only language Israel speaks to Palestinians is violence. Looking
back today on the incident that cost her her right hand and many

years in prison (she was caught throwing a grenade at a military patrol near her home), she says:

> I've never thought of regretting what I did. Every woman has a different idea of her role in the fight. Some participate through marrying and having children, some through studying. For me it was action. We had seen our unarmed brothers and sisters killed, when the occupation came with its planes and its weapons and its brutality. We had to use the same means against the occupation as it used against us. I don't believe the Israelis will give in except to force. And time will show that in the West Bank and Gaza we have a strength that is greater than the Zionists' strength.

Amneh, a *feda'iye* from a West Bank village, was also predisposed to fight by the repression and violence she saw Palestinians suffering all around her:

> I heard about people being imprisoned and tortured, and went to look at their houses when they had been blown up. I was especially affected by the imprisonment in 1968 of Aisha Odeh, a woman from a village near mine. Aisha was the first woman from her village to be educated, then the first woman to be captured by the Israelis after 1967. She and another girl were horribly treated in prison. I heard about it, everybody knew. The Israeli soldiers thought at that time that Arab women, even revolutionary ones, could be terrorised by, how shall I say it . . . Aisha and Rasmiyya were raped, with sticks. It was horrible, horrible.

Despite her awareness, Amneh did not join the national struggle at once, but threw all her energies into her work as a teacher of the deaf. It was the suffering of Palestinian refugees during the Lebanese civil war of 1975 that finally pushed her to act.

> A group of friends in my village started a voluntary work corps that summer. We raised money to send to Lebanon, and did all sorts of things to improve the roads and amenities of our village. At the same time we were studying, reading and discussing together many books about the Palestinian case, Marxist theory, feminism. It was an exciting period, full of work and study and new ideas and personal growth. We were full of hope. When one of the members of the group, who had been in Lebanon and joined the PLO there, suggested we move into armed struggle, we were ready.

Prison

Resistance activity often leads to capture and imprisonment: the country is small, the Israeli intelligence service large, and the Palestinian community riddled with collaborators and informers. Anyone engaging in political, let alone military, activity knows that he or she has to expect imprisonment at some time. Treatment of prisoners falls a long way below the minimum standards set by international law. Perhaps conditions for Israeli civilian prisoners meet these standards, but they are much worse for Palestinian political prisoners who are often punished by the withdrawal of privileges such as visiting rights, exercise and social time. Men prisoners probably suffer more than women, partly owing to the much larger numbers of men. Women rarely number more than fifty at any one time and are usually held in the only prison for women in Israel, sharing premises with Israeli civilian prisoners. Male prisoners, of whom there were regularly a couple of thousand before the *intifada*, are held in prisons in the occupied territories, separated from Israelis' view and more vulnerable to ill-treatment.

Torture is used routinely in the interrogation of men and women. (No corroborative evidence is available, of course, but judging from the affidavits of their clients, lawyers estimate that as many as 90 per cent of convictions in security cases are based on confessions obtained as a result of torture or intimidation. Large numbers of prisoners are held under administrative detention and never brought to trial, so torture does not have to be used against them.)

Interrogation

Hind, the daughter of Umm Hatem (see Chapter 2), was recruited into an underground military unit in Jerusalem after emerging as leader during a demonstration in her school. She was seventeen when she was arrested:

> Someone in another unit was arrested, and he gave away the name of the leader of mine. Our leader just had time to call us all together – it was the first time I had seen the others – and say to us, 'The Israelis have found out about us. You must all escape to Jordan before tomorrow. Except you, Hind, they don't know about you.' I thought we would all be all right. I didn't find out until much later that they had caught him crossing the border that night, shot him in the arm, and tortured him so much that he gave them my name. He told me later that he didn't know he had done it, he was almost unconscious at the time. But he did, and thirty soldiers

came to our house one night to fetch me. My poor parents! There was a
loud hammering at the door. 'Police! We want Hind!' My brother Hatem
opened the door, and there were soldiers wherever you looked, in the
courtyard and on the roof-tops all around. My mother was stirring some
soup in a pot on the stove. She didn't stop, she was so shocked she just
carried on stirring, all the time I was getting dressed. I asked her,
'Mother, it's cold, where are my socks?', but she didn't say a word. They
took my father in, too, for questioning, and as we left the house he
whispered to me, 'Don't be afraid, don't admit anything'. Then he
asked, 'Have you really done anything?', but I couldn't answer him,
because of all the soldiers sitting in the truck with us.

My interrogation began. First the investigators tried to demoralise me
by letting me hear the voice of my father shouting, 'Please, my daughter!
They're killing me! For your brothers' sake, help me!' In fact it wasn't
really him, it was an actor on a tape recording, but I'd never heard my
father's voice shouting and crying like that so I didn't know it wasn't him.
All they actually did to him was to tell him he couldn't go back to his job
(in a big hotel on the Israeli side of Jerusalem, the King David), then they
let him go. I didn't find this out for three months, because when you are
under investigation you are not allowed to see anyone.

Then the investigators called me by my group code-name. This was a
shock: how could they know it? I was sure, you remember, that all my
comrades and my leader were safely over the border in Jordan. I wasn't
prepared for shocks like that. I didn't know anyone who had been
through interrogation, and so though I knew in general that I had to say
'No' to everything, I wasn't prepared for the psychological tricks they
play, especially on girls. My leader should have warned me, but he
hadn't. 'No, I don't know anything. No, I'm not like that. No, I don't
know that person. No, that's not my name.' No was the only word I
knew.

You have eight interrogators at once. Really, how nice! Eight men all
at once, when until then you have never been allowed to talk to one!
They are carefully selected: some of them were handsome, some of them
looked like something out of a horror film.

They sat me on a chair in a small dark room. One of them would come
and grab my hair and shake my head, one would hold my mouth open,
others came and spat into it. 'OK, spit it out!' 'No', I said, 'I won't, I'll
swallow it', and I did. That was the beginning. Then they cursed me,
called me a prostitute, said they would spread it all over the newspapers
that they had found me pregnant, so that my family would disown me.
But that didn't affect me. I knew I wasn't pregnant, and said so.

They beat me with a stick, a very flexible cane, on my stomach. Every
night I lost consciousness, and would come round to find the doctor
beside me. Then one day they told me to take my clothes off. This was
the first thing I found myself unable to do. I was shaking. A big dark ugly
man came in with a stick, and I knew he was going to rape me with it.

'Please don't! I'm young!'

'Are you going to take your clothes off, or am I?'

'OK', I said, and started to undress.

'You're not afraid?'

'No', I said, because I could see now that he wasn't going to do anything. His orders were just to frighten me. All eight interrogators came in, to fondle me, laugh at me, touch my breasts. I was so ashamed, because all I could do was hold my hands over my pubis.

Another method the interrogators used with me was isolation. I was put to stand in a tiny cell, and whenever I started falling asleep the guards threw cold water in my face. After five days, when I was weak from lack of food and sleep, they took me to another small room with a window and left me there alone. I went to look through the window – and saw my leader, with a bandage round his arm, in another room below me with two interrogators. I didn't believe it was him. I'd been thinking he was miles away in Jordan. But the guards took me round to the door so I could see his face. I realised that it really was him, and understood what must have happened.

There was worse to come. I was taken to another small dark room, where I found my leader sitting with one of the interrogators I particularly hated. He was known as Abu Salem. There was an empty chair between them for me. Abu Salem spoke to my leader: 'Tell her not to be such a heroine. Tell her what you've told us, that she's your leader, that she planted the bomb in the Jaffa Road supermarket, that she has a gun. Tell her that if she admits these things, she'll get a lighter sentence.' Hearing all this from Abu Salem was nothing, but when my leader himself said, 'Please, Hind, say what he wants you to', then . . . You know, he'd been like a father to me, that man, like the ultimate *feda'i*, almost like God. I couldn't believe what I was hearing. 'What do you mean? I don't know who you are', was all I could say. 'No, Hind, please. It's for your own good. I know what they've been doing to you. You must think of yourself now.'

My leader! I can't explain what happened to me then. Everything collapsed, everything. I jumped up and grabbed his wounded arm and squeezed it until the blood came. He didn't flinch. I wanted to show him that I was strong, that he mustn't be afraid for me. I wanted him to take back his words.

I was taken back to isolation for a while, then the interrogators started on me again. 'Now you will talk.' This time it was a famous one called Abu Hani. He was an old man, handsome, with green eyes and a distinguished face, white hair and a white beard and white hair on his chest. Even in winter he wore just a shirt, unbuttoned. He hardly spoke a word to me. 'Do you want to talk or not? Before I finish lighting this cigarette, you must say you'll confess.' Prisoners know what this means. It's the most frightening thing. But I repeated, in a gentle voice, 'I've got nothing to say'. I was thinking, 'Perhaps because he's an old man he'll be kind to me'. I was wrong. 'Take your clothes off. Not your trousers. Put your hands behind your back. I want to see your breasts.' And he picked up his stick and slashed at me.

I lost consciousness, and didn't know anything else until I woke up four days later in the hospital. It's not really a hospital, just a corner of the prison where they sew up people who have been tortured too much. I found that Abu Hani had cut one of my breasts open, and the doctors had sewn it up again. 'Thank you', I said when I came round. I was changed, though. Whenever I saw anything red after that, I thought it was blood and panicked.

Now the investigators began to feel they were getting somewhere with me. Back I went to my eight friends. 'Now we think you'll talk.' I didn't answer. 'Will you or won't you?' One of them got up and came over to me and was going to hit my breast . . . 'Give me the paper, I'll sign it.'

They were so happy! Maybe they would all be promoted to colonel! They brought me a piece of paper and I wrote, 'I am a member of the Popular Front for the Liberation of Palestine'. Is that all? That's not enough, they want bombs, attacks, everything, they knew it was a military cell I belonged to. They were furious. 'What's the use of this? We know this already. Give us something serious!' They saw they were going to have to start the investigation all over again.

Now they made their first mistake. It was stupid of them. Didn't they see how weak I was? If they had pushed me further then, I might have said whatever words they put into my mouth. But one of them said, 'Let's send her into the prison with the other girls for a few days. Let her rest a bit, then she'll come back and talk to us, because she knows what we'll do if she doesn't.'

To be with the other girls, to hear their stories, it was wonderful! After two days with them I had regained all my courage. I came back to face the investigators again, saying, 'I've told you everything I know. Do what you like to me, I can't tell you any more'.

'We'll send you back to Abu Hani.'

'Go ahead, here's my other breast.'

The beating, the spitting, everything started again. But I'd been in for two months now, and when my leader came back to himself and retracted everything he'd said under torture, the interrogators gave up. They decided they'd have to be content with sentencing me for membership of the PLO. None of them would get his promotion!

They sent for my lawyer. She was the first person from outside who had been allowed to see me in all this time. Not even the Red Cross had been let in. I had caught a glimpse of my mother once, but not been allowed to speak to her. It was when I was being taken across one day from the prison to the court-room for a hearing to extend my detention. I heard my mother crying 'Oh my daughter!' and saw her in the yard. She had been coming every day to the prison and asking to see me. She ran towards me, crying, 'Let me touch her! I want to touch her!', but the guards pushed me on.

Because imprisonment is such a common result of resistance, and because in prisons the confrontation between powerful oppressor and oppressed is enacted in concentrated form, prisons have become focal points of the Palestinian resistance movement in the occupied territories, and figure largely in its imagery. Prisoners are acclaimed as national heroes. Their refusal to accept humiliation from the prison regime is a statement of defiant national pride which is almost as central to the mythology of the resistance as 'martyrdom' (that is, death at the hands of Zionist forces). The prison system is jokingly called 'the revolutionary university', from the support the prisoners give each other and the highly organised study programmes they often set up for themselves. Hind speaks with what almost seems like nostalgia of the four years she spent in prison. She found among the Palestinian political prisoners a spirit of camaraderie, openness and supportiveness which she has never been able to recreate outside.

Despite the positive image of prisoners in general, the imprisonment of girls is popularly associated with shame, and especially with rape. As the number of women going through prison grows, however, this connection is being weakened. Female prisoners themselves are able to deal more confidently with the sexual threats that are routinely made to them during interrogation, as Hind demonstrated, and their families feel less dishonoured.

The negative image of prison is still powerful, however. Amneh describes her feelings as she arrived at Neve Tirza women's prison after a month of severe ill-treatment in the Muscobiyye interrogation centre in Jerusalem:

> I'll never forget the day I was taken to Neve Tirza. It was 15 December 1977. I was frightened. I had in my mind a picture of prison as the kind of terrible place you see in old films. I knew my heroine Aisha was there, and because I had heard so much about her torture and suffering I pictured her as a white-haired old lady in a wheel-chair. When I arrived and actually saw her, young and active, with shining eyes and full of energy, I realised that prison was going to be all right! I was so happy to see how powerful and enthusiastic all our women in prison were, I said to myself, 'I am lucky to have this opportunity to know and learn from these wonderful revolutionary women'.

Resistance in prison

In the eight years she served, Amneh learned how the prisoners could use their utmost resources of personal strength and will to withstand the dehumanising prison regime. On Aisha's release,

Amneh, with one or two others, inherited her position of leadership.

> Re-assessing one's past, as one does in prison, can be very difficult. I realised that my Christian upbringing and my character had made me very passive, ready to like everybody. In prison I saw that I had to change this. It's difficult to go on being a good Christian when you've decided you must be strong. 'Love your enemy' – why should I? 'Turn the other cheek' – you wouldn't last long in prison if you did that! Not accepting passively is the essential thing in prison. Directly or indirectly, the intention of the prison regime is to force you to surrender to your circumstances. Prison wants to take away your independence, your human personality. To keep yourself alive, you have to keep giving things out from yourself all the time, even though the authorities are trying to snatch everything away as it comes. I'll give you an example: to pass the time and decorate our surroundings, we used to sew our blankets together to make quilts. Every month, when the guards inspected the cells, they unpicked our work. Every month we sewed them up again. We refused to give in. The warden couldn't believe it.

Prisoners are constantly aware of the important role they play in maintaining their people's will to resist.

> If we prisoners are strong, our people are strong. If they are strong, we are strong. Our families come and see us, and when they see what a good mental and physical state we are in, even though we are in prison, it strengthens them. They are proud of us and of themselves.

This sense of purpose unifies the prisoners in their defiance of the prison authorities.

> Struggle in prison forces you to reach downwards to the roots of yourself, to what is basic and essential. You stop thinking of yourself as an individual and think only of the group. You feel that you are the Palestinian liberation movement, the prison authorities are Zionism, and it is up to you to prove that Palestine cannot be reduced to feeble helplessness.

Women prisoners have been able to develop this exhilarating cohesiveness as a weapon. They made victorious use of all the limited tactics available to them during a nine-month strike from June 1983 to March 1984. According to Israeli lawyer Felicia Langer, their strike was more significant than many similar strikes mounted by men:

It was not a mere reaction to a bit of Israeli brutality, it was a clearly thought-out, principled political stand, and entirely the prisoners' own initiative. They were ahead of the men's prisons in doing this. Their struggle was so heroic, it was one of the most inspiring pages in the Palestinians' struggle for dignity.

The aim of the strike was to gain *de facto* recognition that Palestinian prisoners, who are imprisoned for security offences such as membership of the outlawed PLO, are political prisoners, distinct from the Israeli prisoners held in the same gaol for civil and criminal offences. The Palestinian women began by refusing to clean and cook for their guards. They were punished by the suspension of family visits, confinement to their cells for twenty-three hours a day, and denial of all recreational activities. It was their library that they most minded losing, as Amneh describes:

We said to ourselves, 'Books are our spiritual food. We believe and all the world believes that prisoners have the right to books.' So we used to sneak books off their shelves in the dining-room and smuggle them under our jerseys to our cells.

After five months of this, the warden determined to assert her control, and the prisoners were disturbed one night by the sound of their books being dragged away along the corridor in sacks.

We started to bang on our doors shouting, 'Bring back our books!' Ten minutes later the section was full of soldiers wearing gas masks, spraying tear-gas at us. We went on with our chanting, and started singing Palestinian songs. More troops were called in, until there were sixty of them, to deal with thirty-five of us. The small cans of gas were having no effect, so they brought tanks of gas and turned hoses on us. Picture the cell-block: two rows of cells with a corridor between them, windows to the corridor and to the outside. Soldiers surrounded the block and filled the corridor, and poured gas into the cells from both directions – not ordinary tear-gas now, but a thick, burning, yellow cloud. I think it must have contained sulphur, but as far as I know no one has ever found out exactly what it was.

It was like a scene from hell, the air thick with fumes, the girls choking and retching and falling screaming on the floor, panic and confusion, the religious ones among us calling out verses from the *Koran* and committing themselves to Allah because they thought they were about to die. How long the attack lasted I've no idea. When it was over the gas had precipitated into a yellow liquid that lay thickly on every surface. Some of the girls lay collapsed where they had fallen. I didn't sleep that night. I sat on my bunk and from time to time called out to the others, 'Therese, Nahla, Majida, are you all right?' They felt 'Amneh is OK, I am OK, we will survive'.

Now, we hadn't discussed this with each other at all, but when the warden came the next morning and said 'Good morning' to us, nobody answered her. Like one woman, we refused to speak to her. 'How are you?' Not a word.

The gas clung for months to the paintwork and blankets in the cells, and its after-effects were long-lasting and painful – burning, vomiting, choking and sore throats. The guards wore gas-masks in the block for a week afterwards, while the prisoners were still locked in their cells with no escape and no protection. But they refused to beg for mercy, and their continued silence wore down the warden's spirit. Amneh goes on:

> She was the warden, she wanted to have control over us. But controlling people needs their co-operation. Speaking to people and having them obey you, that is the process of control. We knew that a character like hers couldn't bear to be powerless.
>
> On March 7th, we decided to escalate our strike. The situation was mature. Public opinion in the occupied territories and in Israel was completely with us. Our resistance had drawn such widespread public attention and sympathy that the Israeli authorities were trying to suppress all news about us. They realised that every person who read about our sufferings would be a new recruit for our cause, a witness against the authorities' brutal actions. Of course, it was particularly because we were women that we attracted so much sympathy. It was something new for women to be so strong, and the public feels – wrongly, of course – that though men can endure it, women should not be treated with such brutality. We didn't mind if our sex was useful in recruiting more people to support prisoners' rights.
>
> We began our hunger strike on March 7th. On the 8th, the warden sent for me and another woman who were the spokeswomen for the rest, and said, 'You are not obliged to work for the guards'. So our nine months of struggle was over, on International Women's Day.

Two months after this, in May 1985, eleven long-term women prisoners, including Amneh and Salwa, were released along with over a thousand men in exchange for six Israeli soldiers held captive by a section of the PLO in Syria. Will Amneh be able to put what she learned of leadership and struggle in the closed world of prison to use in the more diffuse and distracting world outside where everyone has more to lose? She feels that she has found a way of doing so:

When I came home, after seven years away, I felt like a plant that has been put into the right soil. A new phase of my life has begun. My job is still important to me – the ability to give words to children without the power of speech is a gift I will never despise – but it will not take up my whole life as it used to; nor do I feel that 'job' and 'struggle' are exclusive choices. I can see my work in the context of the national struggle.

Amneh has not necessarily rejected armed struggle, but perhaps doubts its relevance to the situation in the occupied territories. She is certainly not content, on the other hand, to sit and wait for a solution to be devised by politicians elsewhere:

I know exactly what I can do and what the limits of my accomplishment must be. The most important thing I have done since I came out of prison is join one of the women's committees.

The women's committees movement aims at mobilisation on a broad scale. It wants to help Palestinian women help themselves, developing their communal strength and individual confidence. Amneh sees this kind of gradual development as the essential underpinning without which more dramatic and sudden changes, political or social, will be hollow:

A German comrade in prison used to say, 'The old tooth will fall out of its own accord when the new one has grown to replace it'.

The growing strength of the Palestinian people will give substance to their demands for a political solution, and socially women will be better prepared when a solution is reached to take their places as equal members of the new society.

10

Women's organisations

As questions of personal status and social roles are inseparable from the struggle for national liberation for Palestinian women, there are no clear demarcation lines separating the various aims of the women's organisations. Older societies tend to stress charitable welfare provision; the newer committees place emphasis on the achievement of personal autonomy and democratic responsibility. But throughout the twentieth century, women's concerns have not been isolated from national affairs, and with varying emphasis most of the women's organisations have had as their overriding goal the development and strengthening of the Palestinian people.

The first women's societies

From the early 1920s a few women were able to form themselves into organisations and participate in the public life of the nation, encouraged perhaps by similar nationalist-feminist societies that were developing in neighbouring Egypt, Turkey and Syria. The members of these early groups were women of the urban bourgeoisie, who had the advantages of education and freedom from household chores. Many belonged to Palestine's prominent political families. The earliest societies originated in charitable impulses, but education and improvement in the lot of women were among their aims. As the threat to Palestinians from Zionism and British mandate policies became more acute, political activities often took priority. In 1929 the first nation-wide women's meeting was called to express women's horror at the mandate troops' harsh suppression of popular riots against Zionist immigration. From this meeting arose a permanent national women's committee explicitly committed to the nationalist aim of 'supporting any national body in any enterprise which may be beneficial to the country, whether economically, socially or politically'. To make their voices heard on the political stage, these women had no choice but to defy restricting social conventions: they spoke on public platforms, marched or drove in processions in the street, confronting armed troops as they did so, removed their veils, and entered the presence of strange men (such as the British High Commissioner) to present petitions.

Coping with the crisis of 1948

The next step forward for women was again a response to immediate practical necessity. After the Zionist victory in 1948, thousands of refugees, orphans and wounded had to be provided for. In the prevailing atmosphere of chaos and shock, women mobilised to help cope with the disaster. Existing societies grew and new ones sprang up. They organised volunteers to provide shelter, collect resources from the community, run kitchens and improvise hospitals. Mrs Hajjar recalls the beginning of one, the Bethlehem Arab Women's Society:

> We founded the society in 1947, when we knew there was going to be a war. The British had announced they would leave, there were some incidents, we could see that first aid would be needed. We were just a group of women living in Bethlehem. We were not politically aware at all: Bethlehem was a small town, and not at the hub of national life like Jerusalem. We had been quite unthinking, I suppose, but once we saw we were needed, we worked very hard. First we invited all the principal ladies of Bethlehem, the educated ones, Christian and Muslim, to come to a meeting, and we started preparing ourselves to give first-aid assistance. Four doctors gave us training in first aid and how to give injections, and we started collecting things to establish a little hospital.
> The British mandate troops withdrew a few days earlier than they had said they would, leaving all the principal buildings of the country in the hands of the Zionists. We Palestinians weren't even allowed to have any bullets. The Arab armies finally entered the country a few days later. There was no fighting actually in Bethlehem, but all around us there was, and the Zionists took the area's main hospital, so all the wounded Arab soldiers, Egyptians, Jordanians, Syrians, as well as Palestinians, had to come to Bethlehem. The two small hospitals here were not enough, and

our little seventy-bed hospital soon filled up. Bethlehem boy scouts went out at night carrying stretchers to the scenes of the fighting, brought the wounded back to the hospital, and then came to fetch us out of our beds to look after them. We had four volunteer doctors and an operating room for them to remove bullets and so on. The local people gave us everything we needed: beds, linen, food. My brother ran a pharmacy and he gave drugs and ether, as well as a big room in his house where all our members came every day to wash sheets and roll bandages. People used to ring us up and ask, 'How many wounded have you got today?' 'Seventy', I'd answer. 'I'll prepare a mid-day meal for them.' The people's morale was high at first. It didn't occur to us that we might lose. But how could we have won? The Zionists had been preparing themselves for years, while we couldn't prepare ourselves at all, the British forbade it.

As the war continued, the refugees came. It was terrible. They had left everything behind, and that winter there was a lot of rain and snow and they were sleeping almost underwater. It was when we saw the cruelty and injustice done to them that we Bethlehem people really became nationalists. We tried to do what we could for the refugees who camped around Bethlehem. We set up a kitchen and for six or seven months were cooking five hundred meals every day. We had sixty members by then, but it was still hard work. Local people could not give us so much by now; they were suffering themselves and we were all very sad and discouraged after our defeat. So the Union made an appeal to the Bethlehem people living in Latin America: a lot had been emigrating there since Turkish times and been successful, and when they heard about the refugees' plight they were very generous.

This essential work made huge demands on women's initiative, powers of leadership, and organisation. It established for the women's societies a permanent place in national life. Their role changed, as the Red Cross and then the United Nations Relief and Works Agency (UNRWA) took over the task of providing basic necessities for the refugees. The women's societies turned their energies to satisfying longer-term needs. When Jordan annexed the West Bank in 1950, it found women's and other charitable societies running a variety of essential welfare institutions – orphanages and children's homes, clinics and old people's homes, centres for the handicapped, welfare assistance and educational loan schemes. By the mid 1980s there were nearly one hundred societies registered as members of the Union of Charitable Societies and receiving support from Jordan's Ministry of Social Welfare. These are not all women's associations, but women form a large part of their total membership. In the absence of a national government the societies still have an important responsibility.

Out of the hurried emergency arrangements of 1948 (and 1967, when another war produced new disruption and a new wave of refugees) grew several important institutions whose leaders are respected national figures. Dar el-Tifl is one example. Founded by the daughter of a prominent family, Hind Husseini, to care for orphans who survived the massacre of Deir Yassin in 1948, Dar el-Tifl now includes a school, a university college for the training of teachers and social workers, and a museum of national culture and costume, in addition to the orphanage.

From the perspective of women's progress towards equality, this generation of women's societies represents a significant and necessary but limited step. Valuable and respected, important and autonomous though it is on the national stage, much of the work of these societies is still in a special 'women's sphere' which does not present a fundamental challenge to the traditional perception of women. However, one should not underestimate its value from a feminist point of view. For hundreds of middle-class women 1948 was the first time they had stepped out of their sheltered domestic life to join in a vital communal activity. Many women continue to find fulfilment in the work of the societies, which provide an acceptable avenue for the exercise of public spirit and power.

The politics of self-reliance

After the turbulence around 1948, Palestinian nationalist activity was almost in abeyance for a decade and a half. Egypt's Abdul Nasser and other leaders with pan-Arab national ambitions were declaring the Palestinian cause their own, and Palestinians, exhausted and weak from their defeat, waited for others to confront Zionism on their behalf. The women's societies in the West Bank and Gaza Strip shared in this quiescence, carrying on their welfare tasks under Jordanian and Egyptian tutelage without any overt political aims. Then in 1965 the Fatah commando group was established, declaring that Palestinians must take control of their own fate and the struggle against Zionism. After years of waiting and seeing nothing achieved, Palestinians were ready to embrace Fatah's policy, especially after Israel's effortless victory in 1967 demonstrated the inadequacy of Arab support for their cause.

Over the next few years the scattered Palestinians were united in a surge of new hope and activity. Women's societies in the occupied territories reflected this revitalisation. Several new societies were registered in 1965, the year of the foundation in exile of Fatah and of the General Union of Palestinian Women. New goals appeared: Palestine's newly-declared national self-reliance was echoed in a shift in some societies away from the kind of welfare work which aimed simply to help the weak survive, to a commitment to self-reliance at the individual level. Samiha Khalil explains the impulse behind the In'ash el-Usra Society, which was founded after 1967 to help the families of men who had died or been imprisoned in the war:

> I saw the United Nations offering charity to our people – the same United Nations that had been so quick to recognise the state of Israel when it was established on our land, and so had helped create our desperate situation. 'The United Nations doesn't really want to help us', I thought. 'It barely wants to keep us alive. There must be some way I could help the war victims provide for themselves.' And in one small room I started teaching women to sew, so that they could work to support their families.

From that small beginning, the In'ash el-Usra Society has grown into one of the major educational and cultural institutions in the West Bank, comprising an orphanage, a vocational training college for women, a kindergarten providing training for teachers, a food production and catering service, a centre supplying knitting and sewing home-work to hundreds of women, and a museum and folk-lore institute.

Contributing to *sumud*

By the early 1970s it was clear that the occupation was going to be a long one, as Israel pursued policies of attrition to try to force Palestinians to leave. In response Palestinians in the occupied territories developed the concept of *sumud* (steadfastness), described in Chapter 9. For the bolder and more far-sighted of the women's societies, *sumud* presented a new opportunity to contribute creatively to the national cause. Mrs Hajjar explains:

We used to give food to the poor in the region, and there were many who needed it, but after the occupation we had a radical change of thinking. We realised that instead of giving charity, we should give work. This was because so many people were leaving and going to look for work outside, we thought we could encourage them to stay.

It was not easy to provide economically viable work, because of Israel's tight control of the economy. Samiha Khalil found, after some trial and error, that it was possible to sell Palestinian embroidery to visitors and abroad; other societies do the same. The In'ash el-Usra Society also successfully processes food for sale in local shops and provides a catering service for local institutions. This creates work for a number of women and brings income to support the Society's other activities. The Bethlehem Society found a different niche:

We offer interest-free loans to anyone who wants to set up a small shop, or buy a new cow, or set up a workshop to make beads and rosaries – these small industries can succeed because we have so many tourists coming to Bethlehem. We also run vocational classes and apprenticeships to train boys in local crafts, like silversmithing. We give loans to students who want to go to university. Nobody has ever failed to pay us back yet. For women, there is embroidery. Women come and collect the work from us and take it away to do at home, when they can fit it in with their housework and children. We sell the things they make at bazaars here and abroad. We can't pay them very well, but it is work women like doing because it's convenient for them.

The freedom the Israeli authorities give the societies to function without interference is conditional on their political quiescence. The societies have to walk a tightrope between, on the one hand, carrying on the nationalist work they are committed to, and thus risking confrontation and closure, and, on the other hand, passively accepting Israeli control. The Bethlehem Society and In'ash el-Usra have different approaches. Mrs Hajjar in Bethlehem feels that important work can be done while avoiding confrontation:

We built a cultural club where we held concerts of poetry and music, and panel discussions on every kind of subject, cultural and political. Now it's hardly used, because the military authorities interfere. We're not even allowed to hold a concert of *Dabke*, our national dance. And if we want to invite a speaker, the authorities demand to know the subject, and how many people will be there. They even insist on coming themselves to listen. We prefer not to hold any events rather than invite the military government.

We go about our work as much as possible discreetly, in silence, so that the occupation authorities do not notice. We have managed to do many things that they might have stopped if we drew attention to ourselves. But it is getting more difficult now to avoid their notice. At first after 1967 they didn't realise what was going on, but now they are more thorough. Of course, they like us to have money coming in and do some kinds of simple welfare work; it relieves them of their duty to provide for Palestinians. But what happens to you if you are outspoken and defiant like Mrs Khalil? She goes through immense personal suffering and the authorities obstruct her work: In'ash el-Usra is not allowed to hold its annual bazaar, the embroidery she tries to export is held up at the border, funds are not allowed in. She herself has been under town arrest for years and cannot travel to raise money. We have not had any of these problems. We share the same philosophy about our work in other ways, but our styles are different. I certainly admire her, and I admire the new women's committees, too. We work with them on occasions, but they are more overtly political than us.

New popular movements and the women's committees

The growth of the popular-based national movement in the occupied territories in the 1970s brought corresponding new developments in the women's movement. A new generation of women – university-educated, politically aware and progressive – appeared alongside the new leadership that was taking power in the West Bank in the 1970s. Like the national movement as a whole, these women wanted a radically new approach to work among women – an approach geared to development rather than charity, to empowerment rather than dependency, to mass mobilisation and democracy rather than oligarchical leadership. With these explicit aims the new generation could not be absorbed even into the most progressive of the established societies: first, because their work needed to be done among the populations of camps and villages, and the city-based societies could not stretch their organisations so far; second, because their political outlook was too radically different and challenging to the dominance of the bourgeois leaders of the older societies; and third, because their openly nationalistic aims could not be pursued in the charitable societies' framework of being registered (and therefore subject to approval) with the Israeli authorities and the Jordanian government. One of the founder members of the Federation of Women's Action Committees, Siham Barghouti, describes the thinking that led to the establishment of the new committees in 1978:

Around 1978 there was a great surge forward in national activity. The student movement, trade unions and professional associations were all getting stronger, the confrontation between the occupied people and the occupiers was intensifying, and this in itself gave urgency and momentum to the mobilisation of women. Women had to join the struggle, one way or another. In 1978 a group of us decided to establish a new type of women's society to work alongside the old ones. Under occupation women have a lot of responsibilities: the children of martyrs have to be brought up, the families of prisoners supported, and so on. The old women's unions and charitable societies meet these needs well, but we felt that a new way of working was needed to reach out to ordinary women, to help them to understand their situation under occupation and overcome their disadvantages as women. By giving charitable hand-outs, the old societies confirm women in their feelings of weakness and dependence. We asked ourselves, 'How will women ever develop and achieve equality with men if they don't have a share in making decisions and taking responsibility for themselves?' By bringing women to take an active role in our new committees, we will be showing them that they are capable of contributing to society. We had read about how women have been mobilised in revolutionary movements all over the world; and we saw how our own Palestinian women were participating in the military struggle in Lebanon. We thought, 'Surely women in the occupied territories too can become a social and political force, a mass movement struggling for their rights?' I'm not saying our task was easy – we have too long a history as a male-dominated society. But we did succeed, to an extent that would not have been possible if we had not been part of a wider movement for democratisation.

Our ultimate desire is for a socialist society but our first goal is the national one. Here the contribution of the Women's Action Committees to the struggle must be understood as part of a long history. The essential fact is that despite the years of aggression we Palestinians have suffered from Zionism and its imperialist allies, despite the severe problems the PLO has faced since 1982, we have not gone under, and we will not. We Palestinian people will in the end gain our independence, so long as we all know what our rights are and keep our minds all the time on what we want. It is essential for the people of the occupied territories to carry on struggling against the occupation, whatever it does to us. The 'Iron Fist' policy of house demolitions, imprisonment without trial and deportations, which was introduced in 1985, has no effect on our determination to claim our rights. Every day more land is taken from us for building new Jewish settlements, every day the economic situation gets worse, but the worse our oppression gets and the longer it lasts, the more strength we find to resist. We have grown up with suffering, we are used to it.

Although, as Siham says, 'these are the struggles of all Palestinians, not just of women', the conventional separation of the sexes and women's lack of experience and confidence in contact with the world outside their homes necessitate separate organisations for women.

Initially, it appears, the newly formed committee, whose members were educated urban women with some personal independence, did not realise the extent of the obstacles inhibiting the majority of women – housewives with little education – from becoming politically active. Only after their initial attempts did they realise that improvement in women's social position was not a secondary goal but in fact should be the priority, both to allow women to mobilise towards national liberation and to give substance to the slogan of democratisation.

> We want to liberate the energies of ordinary working women and housewives and bring them into the struggle beside their more advanced sisters. They need a lot of encouragement. Many of them are struggling in their daily lives against bad housing conditions, poor facilities, and deprivation in camps and remote villages. All of them are held back by the mentality of Arab society, which has taught them that their only function as women is to produce children and be men's servants. We have to fight this idea before we can begin anything else.

Structure and work of the women's committees

It is in their radical democratic structure that the new committees differ most significantly from the older societies. A small group of women in one place form a 'committee', for which the membership fee is small or non-existent, so no one is excluded by poverty. This committee is responsible for its own local projects, but is also part of a nationwide network in which it participates by electing a representative to a regional committee, which in turn elects a national executive and steering committee. Ideas and initiatives can flow both ways, from local committees upwards, and from the central executive down. It is hard to say how far this ideal system succeeds in practice. Many factors make it difficult to follow, among them the education gap between experienced urban members of central committees and ordinary members in villages, and the long Palestinian experience of autocratic rule from above. The committees' desire to expand membership and achieve results also conflicts with their aim of initiating all members into power-sharing, which requires time and patience. But however patchy its effects might be at present, it is a significant indication of the character of Palestinian political life today that the democratic aim is clearly stated and consistently attempted. The rapid expansion of membership is an indication of women's eagerness to participate in some form of social and national activity. The first established of the new committees, the Federation of Women's Action Committees, claimed over six thousand members after its first ten years, and with the three other committees founded later, the total number of women involved was probably around 10,000 by the mid 1980s.

Political slogans and ideological exhortations awaken if anything a hostile response in ordinary women. The committees soon developed a tactic of working through women's small, immediate practical needs, within the framework of traditional consciousness, as a base on which to build women's confidence, ambition and understanding. Many of the committees' projects are services which overlap with those offered by the charitable societies. This does not lead to superfluity, as the inadequate welfare provision of the military government leaves many urgent needs unsatisfied: for example, literacy classes, nurseries and kindergartens, and small-scale vocational training classes. Other activities are of a general cultural and social kind. Craft bazaars with the emphasis on maintaining the traditions of Palestinian embroidery also raise money for other activities. Concerts of music, theatre and traditional dancing are an outlet for creative expression and an opportunity for education, as well as a chance for women to come together to express solidarity on occasions of national commemorations. Some activities are more explicitly nationalist: solidarity visits and practical support for the families of prisoners, rallies, statements of position on political events. Recently the committees have begun to explore ways of improving their members' economic conditions, and the non-profit-making marketing of locally produced domestic goods has proved popular. More challenging, given the economic dominance of the occupied territories by Israel, is the attempt to set up small productive enterprises.

Even in their most traditional activities, the committees, with their emphasis on education for self-reliance, are different from the older societies, both in that each local committee initiates and to a degree is responsible for its own activities, and in that they always try to go beyond the mere provision of a service and use the immediate need for the wider goal of consciousness-raising. Thus literacy classes become occasions for discussing women's position in the family or the latest action of the military government. Sewing classes become the forum for the formal or informal exchange of domestic experiences and discussion of women's social position. Kindergarten teachers try to hold regular meetings with mothers to discuss such issues as child development, hygiene, nutrition and health. If a volunteer dentist visits a kindergarten and examines the children's teeth, the check-up will be followed by a meeting with their mothers to explain basic dental care. Even the least formal activities are significant: the founder of a committee in one small village told me how she had organised a group to attend the committee's national rally in Jerusalem:

> It may not sound like much, but it was a big adventure for us. Of the ten young women who went, I was the only one who had ever travelled to Jerusalem without a man to escort me.

Problems facing the committees

The committees are trying to tackle enormous tasks and satisfy the urgent demands of their members with minimal resources. Kindergartens, for instance, are needed everywhere – in towns, villages and camps. There is no government provision of pre-school education, and voluntary agencies have not been able to meet the need. With their high regard for education Palestinians have been quick to realise the educational benefits of kindergarten classes. More immediately, overworked mothers need kindergartens simply as a place to put their children. This is especially so in the conditions of occupation, when more mothers have to go out to work, families are often scattered and fragmented so that the care traditionally offered by the extended family is not available, and fertility is still high.

For the committees to try to provide a nation-wide network of kindergartens, without any support from a government, is a serious financial, organisational and educational challenge. The committees are not registered with the Jordanian government (because they want to maintain their political independence) and so they do not receive funds as the older societies do. Nor is there much surplus wealth among their members to support them. Lack of funds is not the only difficulty they face. They also have to contend with the shortage of buildings, especially severe in camps. (Constructing new buildings especially for kindergartens is out of the question. It is too expensive, and the Israeli authorities would probably not give permission, as they do not for new schools.) There is very little provision for training teachers, or for training committee members in any of the other skills they need. The inadequacy of transport and communication create extra practical obstacles. All these difficulties are exacerbated by the social restrictions on women and their lack of experience of such major communal enterprises.

At first the committees had to do their best with enthusiasm and hard work, and it is not surprising that the quality of some of their activities was not very high. Siham explains the difficult choice the Women's Action Committees had to make:

> Our critics sometimes accuse us of sacrificing quality to quantity, of being so concerned to increase the number of our members that we are unable to organise them properly or provide good services for them. This is a danger that we are aware of ourselves, and it is hard to resolve it. Reaching the mass of Palestinian women is our *raison d'être*, so we can't slow down or limit our expansion. At the same time, we exist as an organisation for the sake of our members, so we have to try to provide what they want, not what we on the central executive committee decide they should want. We ask our members what their principal problems are. They say, 'Children. If we want to become active, either going to work or becoming involved in the committees, we need kindergartens and nurseries for our children.' We reply, 'We haven't got the resources to establish big kindergartens'. 'But this is our immediate problem. If you want us to get on, you must help us to solve it.' So we think that having kindergartens open is the first priority in this area. We stretch our slender resources to open as many kindergartens as possible, and we will work gradually to improve their quality.

This choice creates another problem: how to avoid becoming just another welfare agency. Mothers do not have much time to spare for their own advancement. Running a kindergarten is relatively easy, compared with the difficulty of mobilising women to take responsibility for it. There is a danger that the committees will slip back into the much easier task of simply providing services, administered from above, and postpone their stated aim of involving the communities' women in running them. Dependency is notoriously difficult to overcome, everywhere.

Challenging the stereotype

The facts of such large numbers of women joining organisations, and learning to create activities and provide services for themselves outside the family network, are radical departures for women. The activities of the committees are not radical in themselves from political, economic or feminist points of view. Kindergartens, knitting classes, embroidery – these bring improvement in women's situation, but they are firmly within the stereotype of women's nature and social role. However, the idea of a far more radical role for women is not far away. Siham mentioned women's role as fighters in Lebanon, which has been a striking characteristic of Palestinian refugee camp society in Jordan and Lebanon since the establishment of the PLO. In that context women have learned to bear arms and taken on many jobs usually regarded as mens' – such as radio communications and mechanics – as women so often do in times of war. The village communities among whom the soldiers have sometimes had to live during training and operations accept women doing men's work. What they find harder to accept is the women sharing quarters and living with men twenty-four hours a day.

In the occupied territories, without the pressure of war, gender role changes are proceeding more cautiously. The absence of any significant challenge to the ideology of the family and the sacredness of motherhood has already been discussed. It was an educated, active and senior member of the Women's Action Committees who said to me, 'Motherhood is the most important work of Palestinian women'. Motherhood, of course, can be accepted on different terms – either that it is women's exclusive business, unfitting them for anything else, or that while an essential part of women's life, it does not rule out other forms of activity. Activists in the women's committees tend to hold the latter view. Siham pointed out to me as an important step forward the fact that most members of the executive committee of the Women's Action Committee are mothers.

There is little pressure from Palestinian women to challenge the gender division of labour. For one thing, there is little opportunity for women to enter men's jobs, since in a situation of high unemployment and low economic development, women competing for jobs with men would arouse hositility. During their first few years, the committees' vocational training consisted of classes in dress-making and knitting, following the pattern established by the earliest women's societies at the beginning of the century. Siham explains why this course was chosen:

> We want ultimately to revolutionise women's position in our society, but you can't make a revolution all at once. For the moment we have to work within the existing constraints on women, we have to start with the materials we've got, so a lot of our work is with traditional women's skills. We run classes in sewing, knitting and embroidery. You could say that in doing this we are working against our aims, perpetuating the traditional perception of women, but we feel we have no choice. Urban professional women may know that sewing is not in women's best interests in the long run, but most of our members believe in it, so we must start there and try to change their beliefs step by step. What would happen if we said to a woman as soon as she joined the committee, 'Sewing is stupid work, you must do the same jobs as men'? It would be such a startling new idea for her, she would reject us completely. In fact, a lot of progress can be made within the traditional types of work. We can teach new and improved skills, encourage women to aim for high quality, demonstrate the importance of concentration and the value of working in groups. Then our members see the possibility of improving themselves, and the desire for change will come from them, not from above.

The committees do not give priority to widening the range of jobs available for women, but there is still a role for them in helping more women gain access to the existing jobs, by providing basic skills training, childcare, and home work. All the committees put economic development among their aims. The goal is to help women become economically self-reliant, ending their dependence on men, and more importantly on Israel, by teaching them locally marketable skills. The difficulty is that dress-making and knitting, the only skills the committees can teach with the limited resources and expertise available to them, play women straight into the hands of the exploitative clothing industry and cannot be regarded as giving them much economic freedom, though the work is the best currently available.

Traditional Palestinian cross-stitch embroidery is often done on a home-work basis and sold through the committee or society to raise income for itself and some for the embroiderers; it is the only income-generating activity of many of the older societies. The most successful of such enterprises both artistically and commercially have been those of Palestinian organisations outside the occupied territories, especially in the refugee community in Lebanon. In the occupied territories, many women's societies are realising that though embroidery has its own momentum as a symbol of the nation's cultural identity, its economic impact is very small. The limited market for it is saturated, and hand-embroidery cannot be sold at prices that bring women more than minimal pay. The more progressive of the committees are beginning to pay serious attention to identifying new fields for income-generation.

National focus on development

The committees' attempts are not isolated. Throughout the 1980s there has been increasingly serious debate in the national movement about the economic dead-end into which Israel's policies have driven the occupied territories. Academics, agriculturalists, trade unions and industrialists are involved in seeking ways to inject new life into the economy, through new products and services, reviving local markets for existing products, and seeking new export channels. The women's committees have shared in this debate and are undertaking practical initiatives to seek solutions. Their scope is limited because they do not have the resources for major new training and equipment, but the more progressive committees are investing in carefully thought-out developments based on existing skills and markets: processing locally grown food, and new, more marketable designs in handcrafts. One or two of the new projects are stretching the boundaries of work acceptable for women. In the Women's Action Committees' workshop, women work with hammers, soldering irons and furnaces to make copper frames for decorative embroidered hangings. In all women's committee enterprises, it is women who are taking the responsibilities for management, design and marketing – all roles generally filled by men.

As they enter their second decade, the women's committees are making serious assessments of their achievements in every field and searching for ways to be more effective. Their potential has increased, as their own growth has necessitated the division and specialisation of tasks at the executive level and has attracted funding from outside. Other institutions in the development movement in the occupied territories are engaged in a similar process of evaluation and consolidation, now that the euphoria of the birth of the mass organisations in the mid 1970s has worn off. The different groups working in literacy meet to review methods and curricula; resource centres are starting to provide the basic skills and data needed for long-term co-ordinated development planning and strategy-making; rural and urban development problems are widely debated. Women are a particular focus of attention: women's study and resource centres are being created, broadening the scope from the local tasks faced by the committees to wider questions of rights and world-wide perspectives on women's economic roles and struggles. Development on every front is a live issue, part of Palestinians' political life, at times even at the forefront of the national struggle in the occupied territories. Channelling the energy of women all over the country who are ready to step out of their traditional restrictions, the women's committee movement is a significant force.

A political platform for women

The final goal of the committees is to mobilise women and bring them into the national struggle. Participation in the national cause includes activities in welfare, economy and development; it also implies a role in politics. How far have the committees succeeded in this respect? On one hand, they are a unique platform allowing women individually and collectively to express their political commitment, and they have undoubtedly brought women on to the agenda of national life irreversibly. Some of their leaders are sharing political responsibility with men in the occupied territories' political leadership. On the other hand, a specifically women's voice contributing to national policy-making is only just developing in the late 1980s. Previously, women had not felt the need for such a voice. Given the pressures towards unity and single leadership created by the Palestinians' situation, there is no possibility of a women's movement developing in opposition to national policies. A 'women's movement for peace', for instance, such as has appeared in Northern Ireland and Israel, is not at present conceivable in Palestine.

The committees reflect very closely the politics of the PLO. This may be good for national unity, but for the cause of women specifically, it can be counter-productive. The year after it began, the committee movement split, and eventually four separate 'Unions of Women's Committees' existed. The splits are along PLO factional lines, and do not reflect serious differences in ideals or programmes for women. Most observers feel that the split has weakened the practical work of the committees, introducing competition, diverting leaders into factional political rhetoric and away from the practical work with women, thus hindering the growth of a strong united women's platform. Siham disagrees with this view, seeing the split as both inevitable and healthy:

> If we were to separate women's social struggle from the national cause, I suppose it might be easier for Palestinian women to build a united women's movement – but what would it achieve? Isolating women's concerns would be avoiding the real problem that faces us, which is the occupation. It is true and unfortunate that the political aspect of the movement brought with it factional divisions, especially as we felt the effects of splits in the PLO in the early 1980s. But I don't think the split matters as much as some people say. It is so difficult to organise women in our society, there is so much work to be done at the basic level of individuals in communities, that the more people trying to do it, the better. If having four committees meant that four times as many women were organised, that would be good. Each union must expand at the grassroots level, while at the same time the leaders are making contacts with each other, and eventually we will all come together in one united mass movement. It is sure to happen, it is inherent in our growth. We have the same problems, the same struggle, the same goals for women and for the nation.

Hostility of the Israeli authorities

Whether because of the committees' explicitly political aims, or because they regard any Palestinian organisation as inimical to the security of Israel, the Israeli military authorities do not give the committees an easy time. The latter view, that the authorities are against Palestinians organising in general, seems plausible: the largest of the committees suffers disproportionately more than the others, though it is no more politically explicit. Several of the leading figures are regularly punished, like the General Secretary of the Union of Women's Action Committees, Zahira Kamal, who suffered more than six years of town arrest, being confined to her home from dusk until dawn. Committee activities, too, are harassed regularly by the quasi-legal methods the authorities have given themselves: magazines have to be published under a different title every year to avoid problems of registration and censorship; rallies are obstructed by not receiving permits until the last possible minute, so proper arrangements are hard to make. The authorities hope to weaken the committees by attacking their purely welfare and educational activities. For example, a kindergarten in the Gaza Strip was closed down on the grounds that it could not be granted a permit because the premises were unsuitable: the secretary of the local committee protested that it was impossible to find suitable premises in a refugee camp, where the houses people lived in were not 'suitable' either; she was arrested for refusing to accept the order to close the kindergarten.

It is not likely that this pressure will deter Palestinian women from joining the committees. From the most restricted village girl to relatively independent university students, young women are seeing in the committees a clear and constructive way forward. An indication of the place they have made for themselves in national life is that after the prisoner exchange in 1985, when 1,100 Palestinian political prisoners were exchanged for six Israeli prisoners, eleven of the fifteen women released immediately joined one of the committees. Amneh's eyes showed her commitment, shining with excitement when she came out of the first annual general meeting she attended after her release.

Joining this committee is the best thing I've done. The women's committees are the way forward for us. They represent the Palestinian people, and I believe in them.

11

Conclusion: the impact of the *intifada*

Throughout the years of occupation, but especially in the 1970s and 1980s, the changing position of women has been a matter of public reflection and debate in Palestine. Their past and continuing subordination, their new responsibilities and new demands, their role in the national struggle and in creating the society of the future, are recurrent topics of informal conversation, public discussion and writing.

From the beginning of the century the threat of Zionism and the increasingly fluid, money-based economy created an environment in which change was inevitable. The upheavals of 1948 and 1967 and the dispersal of many Palestinians to the United States, Europe, and other Arab countries opened the way for new ideas and new possibilities. Women PLO fighters in the late 1960s and early 1970s were heroines and models for a generation of Palestinians, but much of the push for change has come from changing social conditions in the occupied territories themselves. Increasingly educated and independent, women have demanded greater freedom, responsibility, and participation.

The gains so far

Women's situation has changed and will continue to do so. The spread and level of education has increased enormously among women and, equally significant, among men. Educational and economic factors are improving women's status within marriage, reducing their dependence on their husbands and their imprisonment by childbearing and domestic work. The oppression of the *hamouleh* is disappearing, and male honour demands less seclusion of women than formerly. A rising material standard of living, patchy but general, has reduced the burden of women's domestic work and given them some leisure; they have become consumers rather than producers. Women are increasingly free to work, to earn income, to travel outside their domestic circle, to participate in the wider social life of their community. Their actions and opinions are sought in political matters. Many women, left to cope on their own when their husbands have emigrated or been arrested, find themselves with responsibilities for managing the family and contacts with outside authorities that they never had before. At all levels of society women are increasingly conscious of their position, their powers, the possibilities of controlling and improving their lives, their social and legal rights. They are increasingly seeking strength in organisation. Many individuals have emerged as leaders, as political voices, and as professional successes, and act as role models for others.

Women's organisations continue to grow as ordinary women find in them a way to express and satisfy their new needs. The atmosphere of change is reflected in many proposals from academics and professionals for women's studies centres, women's resource centres and women's rights centres. Schemes to mobilise, support and train women are part of the daily dialogue of development and welfare organisations.

At the moment women's desires and demands are running ahead of their actual achievements. More women want to work than are able to get permission from their fathers or find jobs; many women regret the education they did not have; most young women talk about how they would like to choose a husband themselves, but many have no opportunity to do so; many would like to be able to move freely and to speak in public but lack confidence.

One can assume that most of the gains already achieved – more advanced in urban areas and among the wealthier – will spread further into rural areas and the lower strata of society. The overall level of education will not be reduced. Despite the 'back to the earth' enthusiasm of the *intifada*, there is not likely to be a return to subsistence agriculture, whatever economic difficulties a future Palestinian state might face: the country is too small and densely populated, too educated, too close to its industrialised neighbours, too much part of the industrialised world, and expectations are too high. These developments will continue to change women's lives, backed up by the aspirations of women themselves.

Many Palestinians assume that women's path to equality is assured. They see women participating in the national struggle and take this in itself as proof that women have achieved equality. Others have a different reductionist view, a socialist one: that Palestine is moving towards an industrialised and classless society, which will automatically bring gender equality. But how far has there been a real change in the perceptions of women?

As we have seen in these chapters, and as the experience of other countries shows, there is no simple equation between progress for women in particular fields and fundamental 'equality'. This is not the place to enter into a theoretical debate about the relationships between socialism and feminism, property and family, class liberation and gender liberation, industrialisation, consumption and subordination. It is enough to review here those aspects of Palestinian women's position which suggest that they might be progressing towards a more comfortable but not an equal future, as women have in so many other countries.

Joining the workforce: the path to freedom?

Paid work is heralded by many on the left as the necessary and sufficient condition for women's liberation. But work can be gender-divided, hierarchical, and oppressive to women, whether organised on socialist or capitalist lines. Palestinian women have only to look at the example of women in *kibbutzim* in Israel to see how ideals of communal life and liberation from family chores can become institutionalised into a subordinate and little respected role for women. Has any country in the world avoided turning women into a second-class workforce? Women are channelled into low-paid jobs with low skill requirements and little bargaining power – the corollary of the universal expectation that it is women who bear the responsibility for family and domestic chores. Palestinian women, as much as most other women in the world, suffer the 'double burden' with all its consequences in lack of personal disposable income, lack of leisure, and inability to participate in life outside the home.

Domestic life: towards equality?

In the past, before waged work was available, women were restricted to the circle of the extended family, but they were vital contributors to its economy. Now the Palestinian economy is after a fashion industrialised, and the majority of women who do not go out to work have a new role. This has some restrictive effects as well as obvious benefits. With their productive role removed, women are economically marginalised, pushed into the position of consumers on behalf of their nuclear households and given the character of ornaments and comforters of the domestic hearth. Whether this is the fate that awaits Palestinian women depends partly on how the economy is organised in the future, but it is certainly a possibility. One of the ideals of Islamic society, the ideal that the West for so long misunderstood as the actual truth for all Muslim women, has always been the woman who does not have to work and who can therefore remain secluded and 'pure'. A rising material standard of living could be taken as the opportunity for many families to attain this ideal.

A leisured consuming economy can increase the pressure on women to dress and behave in conformity with a sexually attractive and ornamental role ideal. With the spread of Western fashions, cosmetics and advertising, this pressure is already strong in urban Palestinian society, as in other Arab countries. The style of dress desired of women (in contexts where European dress is the norm) is elaborate and provocative; paradoxically it decorates women's lack of right to dispose of their own bodies.

Another result of greater wealth is the trend towards living in separate nuclear families instead of in larger extended family households. This is desired by most contemporary Palestinians, and most women see nothing but benefit in it for themselves. But it too has its ambiguities and dangers: while it liberates young wives from the control of the senior family members, and gives them more power over their household, it does not necessarily free them from subordination to their husband. In a nuclear household, women are isolated and have increased rather than decreased responsibility for the house and childcare. Even the power that women could in the past achieve as head of an extended family – a subordinate but real power – is lost to a woman in a nuclear family.

One loss women have experienced, though I did not often hear people consciously regretting it, is the women's culture that used to be centred around public baths, celebration of births, marriages and deaths, religious festivals and other communal activities. Many observers of traditional Islamic societies have described the rich cultural life of women – songs and dance, storytelling and poetry, prayer, medicine, shared emotion. Higher material standards of living, the separation of households, increased access to domestic appliances, education, modern transport and communications, and perhaps political and social upheaval, have all contributed to the decline of these cultural expressions in Palestine throughout the twentieth century.

An important and generally desired characteristic of an increasingly urban lifestyle is privacy. Within a nuclear family the relationship between husband and wife, and particularly sex, becomes a private affair. In the past women's communal life included some openness among themselves about sexuality – ribald jokes and stories, open assessment of girls as marriage partners for sons, the display of sexuality in dancing. Now it seems to me (though some Palestinian women have disputed this) that prudery, formerly the province of the urban bourgeoisie, is increasing, boosted by the spread of Islamic revivalist piety. One visible sign of this is the decline of dancing: at village weddings today, it is rare to see a woman over the age of nine or ten perform the sexually provocative dancing of tradition, except in the most perfunctory and embarrassed manner. Dancing is 'not respectable'. The benefits of greater understanding of sex must not be discounted, but at the same time it is arguable that the loss of sexuality as a subject for public examination among women, combined with the romanticisation of love, indicates an increasing dependence of women on men. There might be less coercion and violence, but more distortion in the perception of relationships.

The tendency of a consumption and wage economy is towards greater individual freedom, but women are not, or at least not publicly, moving towards greater sexual freedom. As wealth and leisure increase the attainability of the 'pure woman on a pedestal' image, women's communal role as enforcers of moral conformity by means of gossip does not seem to have diminished (although this might be a case of protesting too much, as the reality of control slips out of reach, undermined by new social and economic mobility).

Political participation: a new role?

The participation of women is undoubtedly a crucial element in the strength of the Palestinian national movement, and is valued by the whole community. But as we have seen, engagement in the public sphere of politics does not imply equality in other areas of life. For one thing, women's political role often overlaps with traditional perceptions of women, using rather than challenging images of women's vulnerability and distinction from men. It is possible, though Palestinians do not make this interpretation themselves, that women's actions during the *intifada* have been drawn to the attention of Israel and the world, not because they show 'Look, we are all equal', but because they are evidence that 'even women and children, who would not be expected to behave like this, have been pushed into revolt'.

No challenge to patriarchy

In these three areas – work, domestic life and politics – women are achieving greater power and independence, but perhaps not moving towards fundamental structural equality. What the three areas have in common is the assumption that the natural unit of society is the patriarchal nuclear family, within which women have a natural place, a prescribed and subordinate role in the division of work, authority, and control of sex. This assumption is very pervasive in Palestinian society, almost taken for granted. It underlies the images of the active housewife and the heroic mother. It is behind the ambitions and the actual experience of most active and idealistic younger women, and is the basis of most men's perceptions of the role of women.

Western feminism has analysed the patriarchal family ideal and found in it the underlying power relationships that perpetuate an ultimately dependent postion for women. In the mid 1980s, when most of the interviews for this book were conducted, the Palestinian women's movement did not appear to have made this analysis. Women had not opened up for themselves the option (which they might or might not choose to take) of fighting for a future of absolute equality. They were demanding new freedoms, but their demands were for particular freedoms: to work, to be educated, to choose their husbands. They were not asking for a fundamental re-assessment of gender and sexual relations.

It does not seem likely that Palestine will experience an Islamic revolution like Iran's, with all its consequent oppression for women. Iran was poorer, larger, less educated, less developed. Palestine does not have the conditions for such a revolution. But a new puritanism and revived piety have been features of Palestinian life since 1979; and a re-assertion of the family ideal and a strengthening of the sanctions enforcing family-based morality are not incompatible with the secular politics of an educated, urban industrialised society. The industrial West has seen such a phenomenon, with a return to so-called 'traditional' images of the family, at least in the discourse of the state and big business, and a retreat from sexual freedom and from radical feminism.

Many present characteristics and trends in Palestine suggest that the future for women might be within a firmly traditional patriarchal family ideology. Women would be educated, comfortable, respected and not ill-treated at home, perhaps successful at work, perhaps the companions and friends of their husbands and sharers in economic power and decision-making; but with all this they would still be ultimately subordinate, and every aspect of their lives would be subordinated to their prime role as wives and mothers. As long as the dominant ideology is the patriarchal family, whether the family unit is two-generational or multi-generational, nuclear or extended, women will still be subject to men's control of their sexuality.

Political programmes for women

Many women are aware of the danger that when abnormal conditions of struggling against occupation are over, the return of normality might be a return to the *status quo ante*, with women being pushed back into the home. The example of Algeria is often cited. Until recently the Palestinian women's movement was not devoting much attention to confronting this danger. There did not appear to be any programme of analysing the causes, articulating the understanding, and providing for legislation to enshrine and codify women's equal rights.

Under occupation, of course, there is little Palestinians can do to construct their own reality; the economy, national welfare services and the law are all controlled by the occupying power. But there are political parties with political programmes for the future, and women's organisations with commitments to social change; and the forum of public debate is open to women. Until the late 1980s, they were not using these opportunities to prepare for the deliberate and fundamental challenge to patriarchy that would be necessary in the future if they were to achieve equality.

Such a challenge was not placed centrally, if at all, in the public programmes of the women's committees. Perhaps they avoided the confrontation as a tactic – for fear of going too far, alienating support and losing what they had gained. It might, on the other hand, have been an actual failure to question the norms, either because immediate practical demands and the national question were so pressing, or because of implicit or explicit acceptance of the family model as natural and desirable. Whatever their final objectives, the women's organisations, by their inevitable concentration on women's practical needs – kindergartens, health care, consumption – rather supported the family than challenged it, though they did challenge its more blatant and gratuitous oppressions. There was, in fact, no sign of a radical feminist movement either in the occupied territories or among Palestinians outside. Even in the heyday of the PLO in Lebanon in the 1970s when research institutions, publishing houses and cultural centres were at women's disposal more than at any other time in Palestinian history, no radical theoretical feminism emerged such as exists in Morocco or Egypt.

Women in the PLO

At the level of the PLO leadership, all the major groups within the PLO claim equality for women as part of their programme, but on the whole they have not explored in much detail what this means or how it is to be achieved. Fatah, the largest and dominant group, proposes a welfare state with nationalised industries, in which women's interests will no doubt be taken into consideration; but the structure of Fatah and the profile of its supporters has tended to be traditional, with traditional class and family connections still important. Its political style is hierarchical and centralised, and though it is a secular movement, it mobilises a significant section of Muslim support. The very strength of Fatah is its absence of ideology, and its commitment to nationalism. It appeals to a broad spectrum of the population, including those whose political ideas are unsophisticated, instinctive, conservative emotions of national-ism and tradition. Radical social challenges would be incompatible with the character of Fatah.

The parties of the left are based on Marxist–Leninist interpreta-tions of history. They have socialist aims for the state and the Arab world in general. They lay more stress than Fatah on methods of action: involvement of the people rather than merely leadership, change and struggle coming from below. They tend to attract more progressive, non-religious adherents, and in particular they offer more space to women. However, the numerical strength of these groups is much less than Fatah's, and it is not clear how much influence they will have in the establishment of the Palestinian state.

As for the place of women in political leadership, women form around 10 per cent of the membership of the Palestine National Council. This figure is impressive compared with the number of women in many other nations' governing bodies, but women's participation is not on a par with that of men. They mostly represent the General Union of Palestinian Women, and thus tend to be confined to women's separate concerns.

The Union, established in 1965 soon after the formation of the PLO, played an important role in mobilising women in the refugee camps outside Palestine. To a greater extent than the newer women's committees in the occupied territories, however, most of its activities have been more or less traditional and have encouraged the participation of women in political life as active housewives rather than on equal terms with men. Its feminism is 'soft' rather than radical, working for improvement in women's status and opportunities through positive discrimination, not challenging patriarchy.

The existence of the PLO, with its various civilian and military structures, did give young women in Lebanon who wanted an alternative to the family an opportunity to experiment with new roles without isolating themselves from the community. But this alternative life usually lasted only until marriage. It was seen as an adjunct to the traditional role, not a permanent alternative.

Individual women have risen to positions of power and influence in the PLO, even in military affairs; but as any country knows which has had a woman leader, the presence of a woman at the top does not necessarily mean progressive policies for women. As with any other leader, it depends what her policies are. Apparent equality may be possible for the exceptions, but usually subordination is still the lot of the majority.

The *intifada*: looking to the future

In 1987 the *intifada* broke out in the occupied territories. As it gathered momentum, a new generation emerged as leaders of the Palestinian community. Previous political assumptions were overturned and at the same time social norms were challenged. Women were in the forefront of the *intifada*, drawn by the need for urgent action, the intensity of hope and suffering, and the new openness of society. As the future suddenly seemed closer and more real, women started to ask fundamental questions about the role they wished to play in the Palestinian state and the steps they must take to achieve it. It seems likely that the women's movement will enter the 1990s with new confidence, new clarity and the power to make a profound impact on Palestinian society and politics.

The role of women in the *intifada* has been much lauded by Palestinians, as if it represented a new stage for women. In fact, much of their activity was an intensification and broadening of things women had already been doing. A young woman in Ramallah, some years ago active in the student movement but now kept at home by her baby, remarked:

> If you just look at what's happening on the streets, you might say, 'Yes, the role of the women has changed'. But if you have been living here for the past twenty years, and have been involved in the women's committees and the whole political movement here in the West Bank, then nothing you see here at the moment is actually new.

This is not to say that the *intifada* has not brought profound and probably permanent changes for women. Girls are sharing in the widely-experienced challenging of authority by young people, insisting on the freedom and mobility they need in order to participate. The contribution of women as actors and as leaders at all levels is generally acknowledged; and women's experience as organisers, developed over the past decade, is helping to provide the bed-rock of unified strength without which the *intifada* could not have lasted more than a few weeks.

Hanan Mikhail, a Ramallah academic, describes how she sees the significant steps women have taken in local and national politics:

> The sort of spontaneous actions women undertook from the beginning of the *intifada*, however dramatic, were not new. But gradually more sustained and responsible types of activity emerged, and these have really formed the core of the *intifada*.
>
> When neighbourhood committees were set up (in spring 1988, to organise local support and defence activities) we had a large neighbourhood meeting here and decided that we should elect people, on merit, to form subcommittees for health, agriculture, voluntary work, legal aid, education, and so on. And it was surprising, it was mainly women who were chosen – they had already done a lot of work and proved that they were capable. We had a twenty-one-year-old girl responsible for a major committee in which middle-aged professional men were members; and they agreed to accept that girl as the person in charge.

In many neighbourhoods, women were responsible for most of the activities of the committees. Hanan believes that women also form part of the underground national leadership of the *intifada*, the 'Unified Leadership of the Uprising', which plans tactics and issues orders through fortnightly secretly-produced leaflets.

> This is a very important step, a qualitative change. Women are in co-ordinating groups, and in the information effort, and writing and analysis, and also in the political leadership. Given the nature of the leadership, so mobile, with people rotating and nobody indispensible, I'm convinced that there must be at least one woman in it. And this is really the first time in Palestine politics.

(Some observers disagree with Hanan, and feel that the language and ideas of the leadership group reflect nothing but the familiar romanticisation of 'women as mothers of martyrs'. At the time of writing, the membership of the leadership is secret, so the question remains open.)

Traditional perceptions of women and social restrictions on them are being challenged with a frequency and intensity never seen before.

The tone of the culture of *intifada* is a youthful tone, the glorification of youth, but it does pay tribute to women. Women are still predominantly seen through their reproductive role, supportive rather than active, but increasingly often you hear at least lip-service paid to women as initiators. Our task is to naturalise this new image, to make it an integral part of our culture, and feminist issues and linguistic structures and perceptions part of our everyday vocabulary. We must end the superficial glorification and romanticisation of the role of women.

Some of the social, personal implications of equality, from sharing housework to control of virginity, are not yet in the realm of public discourse. It's going to take a lot of work. But the *intifada* has produced a new definition of honour, a very positive one for women. The new source of honour is women's political action, not their chastity; it is honourable to participate in the *intifada*, honourable to go to gaol, dishonourable to collaborate. It's an active definition instead of the old passive one, both cause and result of women's political involvement. I heard one boy who was always very possessive about his sister say, 'How can I insist on control over her when she could be my superior politically?' And the fear of contamination that used to be associated with women having any contact with soldiers, that has completely disappeared. On the contrary, it's a source of pride for a woman to have faced the enemy soldier, armed, fierce, male, macho, the whole military machine expressed in one person, and for the woman to have survived the confrontation and emerged victorious. We make a point now of looking soldiers in the eye instead of looking down. We challenge them, forcing them to look down first because we know we are right. It's a kind of physical confrontation, where he has all the physical power, but we know that we have all the moral and political power. An Israeli friend told me that it upsets the soldiers very much: they find it quite uncanny to have all these women outstaring them.

Such a change could be short-lived, exceptional behaviour for exceptional circumstances. But there appears to be a qualitative change in the discourse of the women's movement. Women are confronting for the first time at analytical and political levels the problem of how to conserve the gains they have made. Hanan continues:

I see the *intifada* as a process of acceleration, condensation: it has made the confrontation with the reality of our situation not only imperative but quite shocking. We cannot afford to sit back and postpone things any more. This is it, we've got to do it now. The action itself is there, and there is also an awareness of the danger of regression, the 'Algerian problem'. We know that unless women's spontaneous activity is given a context of theory and ideology, it will not fulfil its potential of transforming women's position in society. So as a result of this urgency which is the urgency of the *intifada*, of this intensification which is the intense experience of the *intifada*, there is an urgent and concentrated need to crystallise a feminist perspective and ideology.

In the past, Palestinian women have constantly demonstrated their capacity, and have organised themselves into a strong movement of committees and so on, but we have always been excluded from the decision-making process. The main pretext has been that the national threat is the primary confrontation, and the women's movement is merely divisive, a distraction. The women's movement itself accepted that gender questions were secondary to political. It did not until now seriously address the question: what is the place of a gender agenda in a national movement? But this prevailing ideology has to be challenged. We have to explain that you cannot fragment rights, you cannot say, 'We want our national rights but we will oppress women'. And now, for the first time, the women's committees are taking up this challenge. There is a sort of fusion, the premise that gender and national rights go hand in hand, and one is not subservient to the other.

In November 1988 the Palestine National Council declared the independent state of Palestine. The state has not yet been achieved, but its declaration is a momentous event for Palestinians. The Declaration of Independence is the basis for a constitution, the premises on which the state will be constructed; and it acknowledges women. The Palestinian state, it says, will be a 'democratic parliamentary system based on freedom of opinion, freedom to form parties . . . social justice and equality, and non-discrimination in rights based on race, religion, colour, or between man and woman'. There is still some ambiguity in the attitude to women, as Hanan points out:

> At one point the Declaration of Independence specifically states equality between the sexes, at another it refers to woman as 'the maker of generations'. That is very symptomatic of the schizophrenia about women in our society. The constitution itself, and the legal system, will have to translate into practice the principle of equality.

Various groups in the occupied territories began immediately to elaborate the details of a practical programme and legal system which will be based on gender equality. These include the newly-formed Higher Council for Women which brings together the four women's committees and some independents like Hanan, some of the women's committees on their own, and Al Haq, a Human Rights monitoring organisation. A statement from one of the women's committees illustrates the new understanding of what is needed for the future of women:

> Women at this stage are entitled to preserve all the gains already achieved on the national level and to continue and escalate their struggle for the implementation of their people's rights, manifested in establishing the Palestinian state on national soil. They must also continue fighting for their liberation and for a radical and comprehensive solution to their economic, social and gender problems. They must also struggle for equality with men in the independent state, which they have contributed to building and establishing alongside men.
>
> Accordingly, it is imperative that Palestinian women continue their struggle after independence, and win key positions in the structures of the state. Particularly, women must participate in developing legislation and a constitution, which will give women equal rights with men, such as the right to work and study, and to liberate women from reactionary laws imposed by the occupation authorities, whether in personal status, inheritance, work and labour, or others.[1]

Hanan is confident that there can be no significant opposition to the new status of women:

> The Declaration of Independence articulates principles, and as long as we base ourselves on these principles we will not be outside the mainstream, the consensus. And those principles are religious freedom and tolerance, democracy, political pluralism and, categorically, equality between men and women.

Notes

Chapter 1   The history of Palestine

1. Estimates of the numbers of refugees vary considerably, and these
    figures are approximate. The United Nations Department of
    Economic Affairs gave the following figures for the numbers of
    refugees registered for relief in 1950:

Israel	50,000
Gaza Strip	201,000
West Bank	362,000
Jordan	138,000
Lebanon	129,000
Syria	82,000
Total	962,000

    (United Nations, 1953, quoted in Pamela Ann Smith (1984) *Palestine
    and the Palestinians 1876–1983* (London: Croom Helm).)
2. The following poll results, published in the newspaper *Al Fajr* in
    Jerusalem in September 1986, show how many Palestinians in the
    occupied territories have direct experience of the military aspects of
    occupation:
    Q: Have you or any member of your immediate family experienced the
    following?

Political arrest	47.5%
Beatings, physical abuse or threats	50.7%
Harassment or direct insults at Israeli	
military checkpoints	55.7%
Property or land confiscation	22.8%
Ban on travel abroad	34.1%
Curfew	74.2%
Demolition or sealing of home	17.6%
Deportation or town arrest	15.7%
Fines by military courts	37.6%
None of the above	6.3%

    (Quoted in *MERIP Middle East Report*, No. 152, May–June 1988)

Chapter 2   Women's position in traditional society

1. *Koran*, 'Women'; trans. by N. J. Dawood (Harmondsworth: Penguin, 1974), p. 34.
2. *Koran*, 'The Cow', p. 223.

Chapter 4   Social change

1. Rita Giacaman (1988) *Life and Health in Three Palestinian Villages* (London and New Jersey: Ithaca Press).
2. Roughly 60 per cent of people in the West Bank and Gaza Strip are under 17 years of age (figure derived from *Statistical Abstracts of Israel*).

Chapter 7   Agricultural work

1. Figure derived from the Israel Central Bureau of Statistics, *Quarterly Abstract*, 1981; quoted in Sarah Graham-Brown, 'Economic Consequences of the Occupation', in Naseer Aruri (ed.) (1984) *Occupation: Israel over Palestine* (London: Zed Books).

Chapter 11   Conclusion: the impact of the *intifada*

1. Palestinian Federation of Women's Action Committees, *Newsletter*, March 1989.

Further reading

This list represents a personal selection from the many books and articles available.

On Palestinian history and the occupied territories

Abu Lughod, Ibrahim (ed.) (1971) *The Transformation of Palestine* (Illinois: Northwestern University Press).

Aruri, Naseer (ed.) (1984) *Occupation: Israel over Palestine* (London: Zed Books).

Cossali, Paul and Robson, Clive (1986) *Stateless in Gaza* (London: Zed Books).

Doumani, Beshara (1987) 'Two families', *MERIP Middle East Research and Information Project*, 146, May–June.

Ein Gil, Ehud and Finkelstein, Aryeh (1978) 'Changes in Palestinian Society', in *Khamsin*, 6, *Women in the Arab World* (London: Pluto).

Gharaibeh, Fawzi (1985) *The Economies of the West Bank and Gaza Strip* (Colorado: Westview Press).

Gilmour, David (1982) *Dispossessed – The Ordeal of the Palestinians* (London: Sphere).

Graham-Brown, Sarah (1980) *Palestinians and Their Society 1880–1946 – A Photographic Essay* (London: Quartet).

Graham-Brown, Sarah (1984) *Education, Repression, Liberation, Palestinians* (London: World University Service (UK)).

Gresh, Alain (1985) *The PLO: The Struggle Within: Towards an Independent Palestinian State* (London: Zed Books).

Hiltermann, Joost R. (1985) 'The Emerging Trade Union Movement in the West Bank', *MERIP*, 136–7, Oct.–Dec.

Hirst, David (1977) *The Gun and the Olive Branch* (London: Faber).

McDowall, David (1987) *The Palestinians* (London: Minority Rights Group) Report no. 24, 2nd edn.

McDowall, David (1989) *Palestine and Israel: The Uprising and Beyond* (London: I. B. Tauris).

Mandell, Joan (1985) 'Gaza: Israel's Soweto', *MERIP*, 136–7, Oct.–Dec.

Metzger, J., Orth, M. and Sterzing, C. (1983) *This Land is Our Land – The West Bank under Israeli Occupation* (London: Zed Books).

Nakhleh, Khalil and Zureik, Elia (eds) (1980) *The Sociology of the Palestinians* (London: Croom Helm).

Owen, Roger (ed.) (1982) *Studies in the Economic and Social History of Palestine in the Nineteenth and Twentieth Centuries* (London: Macmillan).

Sahliyeh, Emile (1988) *In Search of Leadership: West Bank Politics since 1967* (Washington: Brookings Institute).

Said, Edward and Mohr, Jean (1986) *After the Last Sky* (London: Faber).

Sayigh, Rosemary (1979) *Palestinians – From Peasants to Revolutionaries* (London: Zed Books).

Shehadeh, Raja (1980) *The West Bank and the Rule of Law* (London: International Commission of Jurists).

Shehadeh, Raja (1982) *The Third Way: A Journal of Life in the West Bank* (London: Quartet).

Smith, Pamela Ann (1984) *Palestine and the Palestinians 1876–1983* (London: Croom Helm).

Swedenburg, Ted (1985–6) 'Problems of Oral History: The 1936 Revolt in Palestine', *Birzeit Research Review*, 2, Winter.

On Islam, and women in Islamic societies

Abu Lughod, Lila (1986) *Veiled Sentiments: Honour and Poetry in a Bedouin Society* (Berkeley: University of California Press).

Arab Women's Solidarity Association, ed. Nahid Toubia (1988) *Women in the Arab World: The Coming Challenge* (London: Zed Books).

Beck, Lois and Keddie, Nikki (1978) *Women in the Muslim World* (Cambridge, Mass.: Harvard University Press).

Fernea, Elisabeth W. and Besirgan, Basima Qattan (eds) (1977) *Middle Eastern Women Speak* (Austin: University of Texas Press).

Fernea, Elisabeth W. (ed.) (1985) *Women and the Family in the Middle East: New Voices of Change* (Austin: University of Texas Press).

Gilsenan, Michael (1982) *Recognising Islam* (London: Croom Helm).

Graham-Brown, Sarah (1988) *Images of Women – The Portrayal of Women in Photography of the Middle East 1860–1950* (London: Quartet).

Jansen, Godfrey (1979) *Militant Islam* (London: Pan).

Mernissi, Fatima (1985) *Beyond the Veil* (London: Al Saqi Books).

Mortimer, Edward (1982) *Faith and Power – The Politics of Islam* (London: Faber).

Prothro, E. T. and Diab, L N. (1974) *Changing Family Patterns in the Middle East* (Beirut: American University Press).

Rodinson, Maxime (1971) *Mohammed* (Harmondsworth: Penguin).

On Palestinian women, in the occupied territories and elsewhere

Bendt, Ingala and Downing, James (1980) *We Shall Return – Women of Palestine* (London: Zed/Lawrence Hill).

Giacaman, Rita (1988) *Life and Health in Three Palestinian Villages* (London and New Jersey: Ithaca Press).

Giacaman, Rita (c. 1980) 'Palestinian Women and Development in the Occupied West Bank', unpublished article, Birzeit University.

Peteet, Julie (1986) 'No Going Back – Women and the Palestinian Movement', *MERIP*, 138, Jan.–Feb.

Rockwell, Susan (1985) 'Palestinian Women Workers in the Israeli-occupied Gaza Strip', *Journal of Palestine Studies*, vol. xiv, no. 2, Winter.

Rosenfeld, Henry (1980) 'Men and Women in Arab Peasant to Proletariat Transformation', in S. Diamond (ed.) *Theory and Practice: Essays Presented to Gene Weltfish* (The Hague: Mouton).

Sayigh, Rosemary and Peteet, Julie (1986) 'Between Two Fires: Palestinian Women in Lebanon', in R. Rider and H. Callaway (eds) *Caught up in Conflict* (London: Macmillan).

Sayigh, Rosemary (1984) 'Encounters with Palestinian Women under Occupation', in N. Aruri (ed.) *Occupation: Israel over Palestine* (London: Zed Books).

Seger, Keren (ed.) (1981) *Portrait of a Palestinian Village – The Photographs of Hilma Granqvist* (London: Third World Centre for Research and Publishing).

Tawil, Raymonda (1983) *My Home, My Prison* (London: Zed Books).

Weir, Shelagh (1970) *Palestinian Embroidery* (London: The British Museum).

Novels

Antonius, Soraya (1987) *The Lord*, and *Where the Jinn Consult* (London: Hamish Hamilton).

Habiby, Emile (1985) *The Secret Life of Saeed the Pessoptimist* (London: Zed Books).

Khalifeh, Sahar (1985) *Wild Thorns* (London: Al Saqi Books).

Index